LEADER'S
GUIDE

Reducing
the Risk

3rd Edition

KEEPING YOUR MINISTRY

SAFE FROM CHILD

SEXUAL ABUSE

Richard R. Hammar, J.D., LL.M., CPA
and Marian V. Liautaud

YOUR
CHURCH

REDUCING THE RISK 3RD EDITION
Keeping Your Ministry Safe from Child Sexual Abuse
Leader's Guide

©2008 by Christianity Today International

ISBN-10: 0-917463-40-4

ISBN-13: 978-0-917463-40-2

Published by Your Church Resources
Christianity Today International
465 Gundersen Drive
Carol Stream, IL 60188
(630) 260-6200

E-mail: RTRcustserv@christianitytoday.com

CREDITS

Edited by: Marian V. Liautaud

Cover design: Mary Bellus

Text design: Mary Bellus

We gratefully acknowledge the contribution James F. Cobble, Jr. and Stephen Klipowicz made developing the original *Reducing the Risk*.

10 9 8 7 6 5 4 3 2 1   09 08

Printed in the United States of America

TABLE OF CONTENTS

FOREWORD

WESLEY HAD A HARD TIME telling me his story the first time we met. We sat sipping coffee, and he struggled to find the words to describe what had taken place between him and his former youth pastor nearly seven years earlier. Slowly, he shared the grooming and eventual sexual abuse his perpetrator—a man he fully trusted—committed against him. As an older teen when the abuse occurred, Wesley spent years blaming himself for the outcome of this relationship. Now as an adult, he still admits to being rebellious toward his parents. At the same time, he wonders, where was the church? What was their role in protecting him?

We set out to address these questions when we launched into remaking *Reducing the Risk* 3rd Edition. No child should ever experience the trauma of sexual abuse—and certainly never in a church or ministry setting. Sadly, there are hundreds of allegations made each year over incidents of child sexual abuse in faith communities. In fact, ministries, by virtue of their open, welcoming nature, often attract predators looking for a low-resistance environment where they can prey on children.

Since the 1980s, when allegations of clergy sexual abuse became widely publicized, people have become far less tolerant of churches that fail to provide safeguards against child sexual abuse. *Reducing the Risk* was created in 1993, when Richard Hammar, James Cobble, and Steven Klipowicz created comprehensive resources to help make ministries safe from child sexual abuse. Because of their work, countless faith communities have learned about the need to properly screen and select workers, and to implement solid supervision policies for their children's and youth ministry.

2008 marks the 15-year anniversary of *Reducing the Risk*. When we began to revise and update the new 3rd edition, our mission was clear: Create a turn-key kit for churches to implement a child sexual abuse prevention program. The Training DVD, Leader's Guide, Trainee Workbook, and Screening Forms & Records File for Volunteers provide everything you need to help keep kids safe in your ministry.

We know you love kids. We do, too. We've poured our hearts into making this the best training on protecting kids from sexual abuse within a faith community. Our vision is that no child—and no ministry—would ever fall victim to the devastating effects of sexual abuse.

Marian V. Liautaud
Editor

H O W   T O   U S E   T H I S
L E A D E R ' S   G U I D E

Be imitators of God, therefore, as dearly loved children. (Ephesians 5:1)

CHILD SEXUAL ABUSE is a very real problem in ministries today. The good news is that the risk of this occurring can be reduced *if* your church is willing to change both its attitudes and practices.

Of course, making change happen is no easy feat. To get your church on board with the need for a child protection program, church leaders and workers need to understand the magnitude of what's at risk and how they can become part of the solution.

This Leader's Guide will help you promote a safer environment. First, it introduces the reality and the nature of child sexual abuse and why it should be treated as a serious threat to your ministry. Then it provides a blueprint for action.

The Leader's Guide should be used to educate and train the key leaders in your congregation about the need for a child sexual abuse prevention program. Every member of your policy formulation committee, ministry safety team, and/or child protection team, should read this book. In addition, leaders responsible for ministry to children and youth will need this book to effectively train staff and volunteers after they have been trained themselves.

SPECIFIC TRAINING FOR SPECIFIC AUDIENCES

Chapters in this book are designed for specific audiences: Child Advocates, Board Members, Ministry Leaders, and Children's/Youth Workers. The Leader's Guide provides step-by-step guidance on how to train each audience within your church. All lessons coincide with the Training DVD.

On the main menu of the DVD, you'll see "Start Training Tracks." Select this option to begin training the following audiences:

CHILD ADVOCATES AND MINISTRY LEADERS For a ministry to catch a vision for creating and implementing a child protection program, someone has to see the need to ensure safety and present a solution. If that person is you, thank you! You're about to make one of the most important contributions to your ministry and every child in it.

If you're a **Child Advocate**, trying to rally support and learn how to get a child protection program off the ground, Chapter 1 of the Leader's Guide was written with you in mind. Chapter 1, along with the "Child Advocate" training track on the Training DVD, equips you with everything you need to put a child sexual abuse prevention program in place.

Ministry Leaders will be the key people in charge of training staff and volunteer workers in child protection. Chapter 3 is written for the person who will be training ministry leaders on child protection. Depending on the organization of your ministry and who is initiating the development of a child protection program, this chapter may be used by Child Advocates or a Safety Team Trainer. If these roles do no exist, the ministry leaders should train themselves using Chapter 3, as well as all of the other chapters in the Leader's Guide. On the DVD, choose the training track **"For Child Advocates and Ministry Leaders."**

BOARD MEMBERS For a child sexual abuse prevention program to gain traction, churches need to gain support from their governing leaders—board members, elders, and pastors. The DVD track **"For Board Members"** concisely educates your key leaders on the critical need for a child protection program. Chapter 2 of the Leader's Guide walks you through how to present this information to your governing leaders.

CHILDREN'S/YOUTH WORKERS The DVD track **"For Children's/Youth Workers"** is the perfect tool for training staff and volunteers. Ideally, it should be viewed and discussed in a group setting, but when the need arises, individuals can view the DVD at home, following along in the Trainee Workbook, or with our online training at **ReducingTheRisk.com.** (The online training resource is an additional fee). A solid prevention program depends on regular training of any person who works with children and youth. Because ministry volunteers can change frequently, continual training must be built into all youth and children's ministries and programs.

RESOURCES TO FULLY EQUIP EACH AUDIENCE

TRAINING DVD: Ten video presentations are included on your Training DVD. This DVD is ideal for training individuals, small groups, or your entire congregation. The DVD engages both the head and heart, offering personal stories along with practical, how-to teaching. To get started, go to "Start Training Tracks" on the Training DVD. Select the appropriate track for your ministry role. Depending on your role, you may not have to view every segment. Here's what's covered in the videos:

> **Video #1. "Child Protection as the Foundation of Your Ministry."**
> Children's ministry director David Staal introduces the problem of
> child sexual abuse in ministries. This segment gets people invested in
> solving this safety issue by engaging them, heart and mind. It should
> be the first presentation that you view and show.

> **Video #2. "A Victim's Story."** This segment presents the true story of
> a victim of clergy abuse. It should help sensitize leaders to the human
> cost of sexual abuse in ministry settings.

> **Video #3. "Sexual Abuse in Faith Communities—An Expert
> Roundtable."** This presentation features five experts who deal with
> different aspects of sexual abuse in faith communities, ranging from a
> psychologist who helped create his church's child protection program
> to an insurance claims manager who understands the legal impact
> of sexual abuse allegations. By sitting in on this group's discussion,

viewers gain insight into the issues surrounding child sexual abuse in ministries today.

Video #4. "Testimony of a Sex Offender." Viewers will hear from a convicted sex offender. As you'll learn through his story, there's no way to identify who is or isn't a sex offender based solely on outward appearances and impressions.

Video #5. "Screening & Selection: Your First Line of Defense (with Richard Hammar)." Richard Hammar, noted church attorney and CPA, and one of the creators of *Reducing the Risk*, presents a powerful teaching session on the importance of proper screening and selection of staff and volunteers. This segment provides a five-step plan for reducing liability.

Video #6. "Screening & Selection: The Candidate (a short film)." This segment creatively teaches leaders how to interview a candidate, conduct a background check, and check references. Participants will see and hear what the screening and selection process should look like.

Video #7. "Legal Requirements: The Church's Responsibility to Protect Kids (with Richard Hammar)." Viewers receive more training by the most trusted name in church law—Richard Hammar. In this segment, he explains legal requirements for protecting children in your ministry, plus practical tips on how your ministry can meet the "reasonable standard of care."

Video #8. "Supervising Scenarios: What Would You Do?" This fast-paced, interactive segment teaches principles of good supervision. It helps children and youth volunteers think through common scenarios of supervision.

Video #9. "Responding to an Allegation." What would your ministry do if it were faced with an allegation of child sexual abuse? This video depicts the story of how one church handled this situation. Experts add insights to this first-person story.

Video #10. "Taking the Next Steps." Spokesperson David Staal wraps up the DVD and offers action steps your ministry can take to implement or strengthen your child protection program.

TRAINEE WORKBOOK: The Trainee Workbook provides everything your staff and volunteers need to know if they interact with kids. The Trainee Workbook is designed as a companion tool to help you follow along with, and gain a broader understanding of, the material presented in the video training segments. Everyone who completes the *Reducing the Risk* training can complete the Test at the back of the Trainee Workbook. You can retain this test to verify each ministry leader and worker's completion of this training. You may want to have all individuals who work with minors repeat this training on a periodic basis.

SCREENING FORMS & RECORDS FILE for Volunteers: This important tool ensures that key aspects of the screening process are performed and well documented. Inside you'll find all of the resources you need for screening each volunteer who will be working with the children and youth in your ministry, including: a Volunteer Service Application, interview forms with recommended questions, reference check forms, and an area to annually review and update Volunteer Service Applications. The entire booklet is designed to be used as your filing system for all screening information about the individual trainee, helping you keep all critical documentation in a single location.

ONLINE SUPPORT AT REDUCINGTHERISK.COM: This coordinating website offers additional support for implementing the *Reducing the Risk* materials. You'll find all of the video segments online, in addition to discussion boards and a complete resource library. Using the website allows you the ability to train your employees or staff if you don't own the Training DVD, or to train any people that might have missed your scheduled training day. (The online training resource is an additional fee.)

CHAPTER ONE

Training Child Advocates

BUILDING A CHILD PROTECTION TEAM

How to create a team and develop the plan

Children have neither power nor property. Voices other than their own must speak for them. If those voices are silent then children who have been abused may lean their heads against window panes and taste the bitter emptiness of violated childhoods. (Justice Francis T. Murphy)

In most faith communities, there is one or more child advocates—adults who "speak" on behalf of the ministry's most vulnerable members. If you are a child advocate—you care deeply about the safety of children and want to help train your ministry to protect kids from being sexually abused—then proceed with this chapter. By the time you've completed this training, you'll be equipped to train the rest of your child protection team, as well as your ministry leaders. You'll also be ready to begin drafting policies and procedures for your ministry's child protection program. Let's get started:

Training Overview
For Child Advocates (approximately 4 hours)

WHAT IS THE GOAL OF THIS TRAINING?

To provide a functional knowledge of the issues pertaining to child sexual abuse and the ministries, including:

- A clear understanding of legal liability and your ministry's culture
- Principles of legal liability and supervision to help formulate protection policies

WHO SHOULD ATTEND?

All people who care deeply about the safety of children and are involved in the development of ministry policy regarding the prevention of child sexual abuse. This may include board members, pastoral staff, ministry leaders, and other members of the congregation.

WHAT RESOURCES FROM MY **REDUCING THE RISK** KIT WILL I NEED?

- *Reducing the Risk* Training DVD
- *Reducing the Risk* Leader's Guide
- *Reducing the Risk* Screening Forms & Records File for Volunteers

WHAT ADDITIONAL SUPPLIES WILL I NEED TO LEAD THE TRAINING?

- DVD player and monitor
- Markerboard or flip chart, markers

HOW OFTEN SHOULD WE OFFER THIS TRAINING?

Plan to schedule at least two major training sessions per year for new members of your safety team.

Training Step-By-Step

The following Child Advocate training provides a comprehensive overview of the issues surrounding child sexual abuse in ministries and how to prevent it. Depending on your situation, this training may either be used for individuals who want to initiate a child sexual abuse prevention program or to train a group of child advocates so you can work together to form a child protection team. Allow approximately four hours for this training. You may choose to divide a group training into two sessions, or simply take a break in the middle of the complete training.

1. LEADER'S PREP

Whether you're working through this chapter for your own individual learning or training a group of child advocates, select the training track called **"For Child Advocates and Ministry Leaders."** Use this chapter in the Leader's Guide to answer additional questions and read supplemental information. Each participant should have their own copy of the Leader's Guide.

2. GET STARTED

- Welcome group members.
- Ask each participant to introduce themselves and answer, "What prompted you to become part of this ministry team?"
- On the *Reducing the Risk* Training DVD go to **"Start Training Tracks."** Select **"For Child Advocates and Ministry Leaders."** training track.
- **View Video #1: "Child Protection as the Foundation of Your Ministry."**
- **View Video #2: "A Victim's Story."**
- **View Video #3: "Sexual Abuse in Faith Communities: An Expert Roundtable."**

OPEN FOR DISCUSSION:

- What are the major issues that have surfaced in your mind so far?
- Which issues mentioned in the expert roundtable are most concerning for your ministry?
- What should children reasonably expect from your ministry when attending services or programs?
- Many faith communities create mission statements and core-value statements for their children's ministries. Does your faith community have such a guiding statement? Does it underscore your commitment to keeping kids safe physically, emotionally, mentally, and spiritually?

- If your faith community does not have a children's ministry mission statement that includes keeping kids safe, it's time to write one. See Appendix 1 for a Sample Child Protection Policy that includes a mission statement. You can adopt this statement or craft your own.

- **View Video #4: "Testimony of a Sex Offender."**

- **View Video #5: "Screening & Selection: Your First Line of Defense (with Richard Hammar)."**

- **View Video #6: "Screening & Selection: The Candidate (a short film)."**

Screening and Selection is the first step toward safeguarding children in your ministry. It's also your ministry's best legal defense should you ever end up in court over an allegation of sexual abuse. *Reducing the Risk* includes a **Screening Forms & Records File for Volunteers** as a part of the kit, and it is sold separately. This is a key component for ensuring that your ministry will enforce best practices for screening and selecting volunteer workers. Pass a copy of this resource around to show the group. Employment applications and hiring forms for paid staff and clergy are available at **YourChurchResources.com**.

Going Deeper ○ ○ ○ ○ ○ ○
Five-Step Protection Plan

Richard Hammar refers to a five-step child protection plan. This simple plan can become the basis for your child sexual abuse prevention program. Let's review these steps:

1. Adopt the six-month rule. Start by establishing a length of time that any person must be a member of your faith community, such as six months, before he or she can volunteer to work with children or youth. The purpose of this rule is to prevent predators from gaining quick access to potential victims. A predator will be less likely to wait for an extended period of time to gain access to children, especially when he or she can go elsewhere and have almost immediate access. Six months provides a threshold of time for individuals to become better known, and gives an opportunity to evaluate their suitability for volunteer service. Some ministries may opt for a shorter time than six months, but the principle remains the same: *Do not give volunteers who are new and unknown immediate access to children.*

Another important threshold requirement is to develop a process so that you know the motives and character of volunteers before they begin working with youth or children. Some ministries do this by requiring that staff and volunteers who work with kids be involved in the faith community to the extent that other adult members can provide a positive character reference for them. These references should be able to describe the potential volunteer's involvement in the faith community, level of commitment, and ability to serve well. This is especially important in large communities where staff members may not have personal knowledge of every member, yet depend on the recruitment of large numbers of volunteers to assist with ministry programs.

Sometimes leaders ask, "What about people who transfer their membership from one church to another, and who have had a long history of working with children in their former church? Do they have to wait for an extended period of time before they can volunteer to work with children in our ministry?" In such cases—if you have conducted thorough reference checks, interviews, and training—it may be appropriate to reduce the threshold requirement. Remember, the goal is not to thwart ministry, but to enhance it through proper safeguards. The key principle at stake here is to prevent people that you do not know from gaining easy access to your children through a position of service within your ministry.

The six-month rule and member references establish an important threshold for the selection of volunteers who will work with children or youth. Next, there's the screening process.

2. Use a written application. Requiring a written application for ministry volunteers serves the same role as it does for paid employees, although the application form can be somewhat different. In the Screening Forms & Records File for Volunteers we provide a Volunteer Service Application. This is <u>not</u> an employment application. It is a screening tool to help you discern a staff or volunteer's suitability for working with children. A ministry can be just as liable for the negligent selection of a volunteer as it can be for a paid employee. The goal is to document the selection process and to be able to demonstrate that the ministry met the test of reasonable care.

Use the applications included in the **Screening Forms & Records File for Volunteers** included in your *Reducing the Risk* kit (also sold separately).

3. Conduct reference checks. Once the written application is complete, the next step is conducting reference checks. If the threshold requirements are enforced, the application should indicate that the volunteer has been a member of the faith community for a minimum length of time, such as six months, and the volunteer should list two or more other references, preferably from youth-serving organizations where the candidate has served in the past, plus two or more references from other members of the faith community.

Remember, it is not sufficient to list only parents of children with whom the prospective volunteer may work. Predators may work at grooming the parents of potential victims. The reference list should also include other adults. These people should be contacted for input concerning the volunteer's qualifications for working with children or youth. Often this is done either in person or over the phone. You may also use a written form that is mailed to the reference. All of these steps and forms are included in the **Screening Forms & Records File for Volunteers**.

4. Interview each candidate. Use the interview as a time to explore more fully why the candidate wants to work with children or youth. It's also a good time to review your ministry's policies and procedures regarding the supervision of children.

5. Conduct additional background checks. For many ministries, the decision whether or not to conduct a criminal background check will depend upon the scope of the volunteer's service and responsibilities. Remember that risks increase when volunteers have frequent, unsupervised access to children. If a ministry decides that some staff or volunteer positions do not warrant this level of screening, that evaluation and its defense should be grounded in a risk management philosophy that can be explained and defended as reasonable if called upon to do so before a jury. Similarly, if a ministry elects to conduct background checks on staff and volunteers, they need to enforce this practice consistently.

> Tip **If a potential staff or volunteer worker will drive a motor vehicle as part of his or her volunteer service, a motor vehicle records check is recommended. This check reveals the volunteer's type or class of driver's license, any restrictions or violations, license revocations, auto insurance cancellations, accidents, full name, and the volunteer's address at the time of last renewal. Availability of violations information varies, but usually goes back three years, depending on the state involved.**

OPEN FOR DISCUSSION:

- Which of the policies regarding worker selection do we currently use? Which ones can we add to more thoroughly screen potential workers?

- What challenges will arise from instituting more stringent screening policies?

- What other kinds of crimes would disqualify a person for service with children?

Going Deeper ○ ○ ○ ○ ○ ○

Criminal Records Checks

No court, in any reported decision, has found a church liable on the basis of negligent selection for the molestation of a child on the ground that the church failed to conduct a criminal records check on the molester before using him to work with children. That said, churches that conduct criminal records checks on volunteers who work with minors will be in a better position to defend against an allegation of negligent selection than those who do not conduct such checks. It is worth noting that a growing number of youth-serving organizations are performing criminal records checks on volunteers, and this suggests that the court one day may conclude that "reasonable care" in the selection of children's/youth volunteers necessitates criminal records checks. Such a finding would make it negligent for a ministry *not* to conduct such checks. Visit **ReducingTheRisk.com** for more information on the topic of criminal background checks.

EDUCATE YOUR FAITH COMMUNITY ABOUT THE SCREENING PROCESS

Screening programs that are "imposed" on communities rarely work. A better approach is to build support for the program through education. Sermons, Sunday school classes, newsletter articles, teacher training events, and Q & A sessions can all be used to educate, inform, and build support for the program. See Chapter 5 of this Leader's Guide for more ideas on how to cast vision to your entire faith community on the critical need for a child sexual abuse prevention program.

A membership orientation class can also play an important role in sustaining the program over time, and in reducing the potential for conflict. During the orientation, all ministry policies concerning sexual abuse prevention should be explained. Explain the threshold requirements for volunteer service with children and youth. Show each member a copy of the Screening Forms & Records File for Volunteers and review it with them. Later, if a church member is called upon for nursery duty or some other responsibility involving children or youth and is asked to complete the form, he or she will understand what is being asked and why it is being asked. No one will be surprised or caught off guard by the screening policy.

When a ministry initiates a screening procedure for staff and volunteer workers, those already active in children's ministry should also complete the screening process. If you discover that a current worker has a criminal conviction that is considered a disqualifying offense, or has pled guilty to sexual or child abuse, that individual should be relieved of any duties in working with youth or children.

○   ○   ○

In the next set of videos, you'll learn more about the legal requirements ministries bear in respect to protecting children. Part of how you fulfill this responsibility is by enforcing safe supervision policies. Worker supervision is the second major policy area of a child sexual abuse prevention program. Negligent supervision can promote the possibility of abuse and result in legal liability.

- **View Video #7: "Legal Requirements: The Church's Responsibility to Protect Kids (with Richard Hammar)."**

- **View Video #8: "Supervising Scenarios: What Would You Do?"**

Richard Hammar previously introduced a five-step plan for preventing child sexual abuse in Video #5. These concepts were put to the test in Video #8: **"Supervising Scenarios."** Review the following "What Does Our Ministry Do?" checklist as a group. Your answers will help guide your thinking on what should be incorporated into your ministry's child protection plan.

Also, we've included a sample Child Protection Plan in Appendix 1 at the back of this book. This sample, along with the following checklist, will give you a clear framework to customize your own protection plan for your ministry.

Assessment ○ ○ ○ ○ ○ ○

What Does Our Ministry Do?

The following checklist can help you to conduct a quick assessment of your protection program planning needs.

As a group, determine whether each statement is true for your ministry. Statements left unchecked indicate an area that needs attention.

☐ We screen all paid employees, including clergy, who work with youth or children.

☐ We screen all volunteers who work with youth or children.

☐ We do reference checks on all paid employees and volunteers who work with youth or children.

☐ We interview all prospective employees before they are hired.

☐ We interview all volunteer workers before they begin working with youth or children.

☐ We train all paid and volunteer workers who work with youth or children regarding all aspects of our prevention program.

☐ We take our policies to prevent sexual abuse seriously and see that they are enforced.

☐ Our workers understand state laws concerning child abuse reporting obligations.

☐ We have a clearly defined reporting procedure for a suspected incident of abuse.

☐ We have a specific response strategy to use if an allegation of sexual abuse is made against our ministry.

☐ We have adequate insurance coverage if a claim should occur.

☐ We are prepared to respond to media inquiries if an incident of abuse should occur.

☐ We review our program on a regular basis and make changes where needed.

☐ We require all ministry staff and volunteers to obtain advance approval before any activity can be sponsored in the name of the ministry, or take place in ministry facilities.

Going Deeper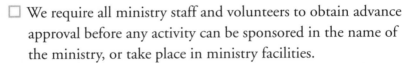

The Use of Principles and Policies

Principles provide an underlying sense of direction, while policies provide specific direction.

When it comes to supervision, many churches struggle with the concept of reasonable care. Often, two extremes emerge. On the one hand, some ministry leaders try to establish a policy for every situation. This rarely works. Plus, like Richard Hammar points out, the worst position for a church to be in is to have a policy and not enforce it. On the other hand, some ministry leaders do nothing. They leave supervision to the discretion of each individual worker, sometimes with catastrophic results.

A better solution is to understand some basic principles of risk. Not all activities bear the same level of risk. As a result, the level of supervision should correspond to the level of risk. General supervision is appropriate for low-risk activities where the potential for a serious accident or injury is low. As risk increases, however, the supervision should become more specific.

For example, while general supervision is appropriate for monitoring children eating a meal, specific supervision is needed for children cooking a meal. By training ministry leaders and workers to understand the principles of risk, they'll be equipped to make decisions as situations warrant.

Three factors affect the level of risk: isolation, accountability, and power. By filtering activities through the following checklist, you'll be able to create supervision policies for your ministry programs.

ISOLATION

Key question: Who will be present for this activity?

▶ *Action step to lower risk:* Increase the number of people who are present to lower isolation and increase accountability.

Key question: Does this activity occur at a time or location that will increase the level of isolation?

▶ *Action step to lower risk:* Change time or location so that isolation decreases, or increase the level of accountability.

Key question: Do we currently secure and properly monitor our facilities to prevent unauthorized use?

▶ *Action step to lower risk:* Appoint a monitor to check buildings and restrooms that should be unoccupied while other activities occur in ministry facilities. Instruct teachers to make sure that the rooms are left unoccupied at the end of class. Have a designated person lock doors and secure specific rooms and buildings at the end of their use.

Key question: Do we maintain control of facility keys, and do we have a policy in place regarding who can use ministry facilities, and under what circumstances?

▶ *Action step to lower risk:* Develop a system to control the use of facility keys. If necessary, have locks re-keyed. Develop a policy that governs the time and location of activities in coordination with proper accountability.

Key question: Do we require individuals to obtain advanced permission before sponsoring an activity in the name of the ministry, or that appears to be a ministry-related function?

▶ *Action step to lower risk:* Require individuals and groups to obtain advance permission from an authorized person before sponsoring activities that are in any way associated with the ministry.

ACCOUNTABILITY

Key question: Have workers been screened in proportion to the level of their responsibilities? Individuals who have frequent and unsupervised access to children require more thorough screening than those who have infrequent contact in group settings.

▶ *Action step to lower risk:* Screen workers according to their level of responsibility in order to determine whether they have been accountable in the past.

Key question: Does a worker have unsupervised access to a child or extended unsupervised access to a group of children?

▶ *Action step to lower risk:* Have two or more non-related workers present.

Key question: Are activities open or closed to public observation?

▶ *Action step to lower risk:* Conduct frequent random observation of activities. For example, appoint an usher to monitor activities throughout the building, or use video equipment to monitor activities. Install windows in all doors, or use "Dutch doors"—doors that are split so the top half stays open while the bottom half remains shut.

Key question: Do workers know what is expected of them regarding appropriate and inappropriate behavior? Do they understand and abide by ministry policies concerning sponsoring and supervising activities both on and off of ministry property?

▶ *Action step to lower risk:* Train each worker with respect to ministry policies and procedures.

POWER AND CONTROL

Key question: Do higher-risk situations currently exist that promote an imbalance of power among children?

▶ *Action step to lower risk:* Instruct supervisors to maintain a balance of power as much as possible in the pairing of children for any overnight activity, going to the restroom, or any other activity in which they may be alone for a period of time.

○ ○ ○

■ **View Video #9: "Responding to an Allegation."**

Video #9 provides step-by-step guidance for responding to an allegation of sexual abuse. All ministry leaders and children's/youth workers should be equipped and empowered to report any suspicion of sexual misconduct. They should also know how to respond to an allegation. To help you, we've included an "Allegation Response Checklist" in the Appendix #3 of this Leader's Guide and in the Trainee Workbook. Review this checklist together and discuss how to adapt it for your ministry.

> **Tip** In many states, both compensated and volunteer children's/youth workers are mandatory reporters. Do not assume that requiring such persons to report suspected abuse to a designated ministry official will discharge their reporting duty under state law. These workers may still have a duty to report the suspected abuse to state officials, as well. Richard Hammar provides an annual state-by-state summary of child abuse reporting laws in CHURCH LAW & TAX REPORT. You can order this bi-monthly resource by calling 1-800-222-1840. Be sure your ministry leaders have access to this report each year.
>
> If you have any doubts concerning your duty to report a particular incident to the state, an attorney should be consulted. It's also a good idea to inform your insurance agent immediately if an allegation is ever brought against your ministry.

■ **View Video #10: "Taking the Next Steps."**

OPEN FOR DISCUSSION:

- Children's ministry director David Staal says that he starts every weekend service by taking a minute to pray for the safety of the children in his ministry. How do you feel about the importance he placed on the connection between safety and the spiritual growth of a child?

- What will you do to keep your ministry safe from child sexual abuse?

3. WHAT'S NEXT?

Now that you've received a complete overview of the *Reducing the Risk* training, it's time to start developing a strategy for implementing a child protection plan for your ministry. Here are specific steps you can take to get started:

1. Determine who will lead the program. Ideally, a successful prevention program begins with people who deeply care about preventing child sexual abuse. You may be one of those people. Others may include a staff member, business administrator, board member, Sunday school teacher, or a person who has experienced the pain of abuse. What if your ministry has no one who deeply cares about this issue? You must still proceed out of moral and legal necessity.

2. Obtain the support of key ministry leaders. If you haven't made a presentation to your governing board yet, schedule a time to briefly educate them on the issue of child sexual abuse and how you can help reduce this risk in your ministry. (See Chapter 2 of this Leader's Guide.)

3. Draft an initial plan. We have provided a sample Child Protection Plan in Appendix 1 at the back of this Leader's Guide. You can use this as is, or customize it to meet your ministry's specific policies. Solicit the input of ministry leaders and volunteer workers to create a sense of broad ownership for both the process and the policies that emerge as a result of your efforts. An attorney should review your policies to see that they conform to state law.

4. Educate workers and volunteers. The next step is to develop a strategy to train all existing workers. Once that has occurred, routines must be established for providing ongoing training of all new workers who begin service in your ministry.

- **Existing Workers.** Schedule a mandatory training session for all existing staff and volunteers who work with youth or children. Since not everyone will be available, a second session should be offered on a different date. Many faith communities use hundreds of volunteer workers in their children's/youth programs. Many of these volunteers may only serve a few hours each year. Practically, it can be difficult to have all of these volunteers attend your training sessions. As an alternative, individuals can view the Training DVD at home, following along in their Trainee Workbook, or use the online training at **ReducingTheRisk.com**. (The online training resource is an additional fee.)

- **Future Workers.** Sometimes, a new worker becomes active after a program has already begun. A plan must exist so that all workers receive proper training regardless of when they begin. Two possibilities for training include giving them the Training DVD to view at home while following along in their Trainee Workbook, or sending them to online training at **ReducingTheRisk.com**, where workers can receive online training at their own convenience. (The online training resource is an additional fee.)

  If you have a new member's class or a class for visitors, provide an overview of the prevention program there, as well. All members of your faith community should be aware of basic policies concerning working with youth and children. Prepare a simple brochure that outlines these policies.

- **Annual Training.** An ideal time for annual training is before the launch of your fall ministry season.

5. Monitor program progress. After the initial emphasis of the program wanes, workers may begin to ignore basic policies. Schedule periodic check-ups to examine the following:

- Has each department trained its workers regarding the plan?

- Are workers following the required policies and guidelines?

- What obstacles exist in complying with the policies?

- What is the level of cooperation?

- Do sufficient materials exist for training and information?

- Are the policies printed and available?

Approximately six to eight weeks after implementation, give a written questionnaire to all ministry leaders and workers to gather additional feedback regarding these policies. Results of the monitoring process should be provided to the ministry board, or to the committee responsible for the ongoing maintenance of the prevention effort. This group can then make recommendations for policy changes, if necessary.

6. Evaluate the Program. Ministry leaders should conduct an annual review that assesses how well the program has met its goals. During this period, ministry leaders should report on the prevention efforts, and a brief questionnaire can be given to workers and representative members of the faith community asking for their reactions and concerns. These reports and anecdotes provide an important source for evaluation. The story of one child spared abuse or one worker cleared of allegations would speak highly of the value of the program. Once finished, the evaluation becomes the basis for reviewing and improving the program.

7. Raise ministry-wide awareness. A child sexual abuse prevention program will gain more traction if you educate and involve your entire faith community. You can do this through a communication strategy. For example, designate one Sunday to introduce the issue. Develop a theme that will challenge and enlist people, such as "Children—Our Most Valuable Gift" or "Responding to the Problem of Child Sexual Abuse."

Since this issue touches people at a deep emotional level, careful planning should be done in advance. You may consider dismissing children prior to the sermon or presentation on the topic. Also, be aware that some members of your faith community may be adult survivors of abuse, so it's important that you recognize the pain associated with this topic. The pastor may find a number of adults seeking counseling afterward, for example. Resources should be in place to respond to questions and personal needs that may surface in the days and weeks that follow.

God has given us a great responsibility to care for our children. Use Scripture verses to highlight this mandate. The following passages may be helpful: Psalm 78:1–6; Psalm 127; Psalm 46:1,6; 2 Samuel 13; Matthew 18:1–6; Matthew 18:10; Luke 18:15–17; and Ephesians 5:11–13.

Introducing the topic of child abuse and the prevention plan may elicit a variety of reactions among members of your faith community. Many will be in favor of the concept. Others will have questions and reservations. Provide opportunities for people to give feedback. The topic can also be discussed in small groups or home fellowships. Have staff members or other ministry leaders available who can alleviate concerns and provide specific answers about the child sexual abuse prevention plan.

Chapter Two

Training
Board
Members

GAINING THEIR
SUPPORT

How to build momentum from the top down

But if anyone causes one of these little ones who believe in me to sin, it would be better for him to have a large millstone hung around his neck and to be drowned in the depths of the sea. (Matthew 18:6)

Until a ministry's board members are convinced of the need to reduce the risk of child sexual abuse, little progress can be made in establishing a prevention program. Education is the key to building support from the top down. Many board members don't see the urgent need for a child protection program because they don't fully understand the legal liabilities their ministry faces.

Fortunately, the *Reducing the Risk* Training DVD is designed to educate governing leaders to respond to the need for protecting children. The training track—**For Board Members**—will remind governing leaders of the precious gift God entrusts to ministries that serve children.

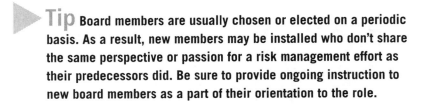

> Tip **Board members are usually chosen or elected on a periodic basis. As a result, new members may be installed who don't share the same perspective or passion for a risk management effort as their predecessors did. Be sure to provide ongoing instruction to new board members as a part of their orientation to the role.**

Action Item:

The pastors and lay people who make up your ministry's governing board are often busy people. This must be taken into account as you develop your educational strategy. Initially, it may be difficult to schedule a special meeting with adequate attendance in order to discuss the subject of child sexual abuse—but don't give up. Try incorporating an orientation session into a regularly scheduled leadership meeting. In such sessions, you'll need only to give a brief overview of the critical need for a child sexual abuse prevention program. Then view the **"For Board Members"** training track on the *Reducing the Risk* DVD, using this chapter as your guide.

> ▶ Tip This overview training may be the first time many of your ministry's board members will be exposed to the details of this topic. Focus the session on the major issues and avoid getting caught up prematurely in discussing the details of a future risk management program. The goal is to help leaders understand the risk of child sexual abuse, and the need to do something about it. The details of what should be done can be worked out later.

Training Overview

For Board Members (approximately 90 minutes)

WHAT'S THE GOAL OF THIS TRAINING?

- To inspire elders and governing board members to protect children out of love and care for them.
- To raise awareness about the liability a ministry faces with the issue of child sexual abuse
- To motivate elders and governing leaders to implement a child protection program.

WHO SHOULD ATTEND?

- Pastoral staff, church or ministry board members, elders, and key administrative leaders of programs.

WHAT RESOURCES FROM MY **REDUCING THE RISK** KIT WILL I NEED?

- *Reducing the Risk* Leader's Guide
- *Reducing the Risk* Training DVD

WHAT ADDITIONAL SUPPLIES WILL I NEED TO LEAD THE TRAINING?

- DVD player and monitor
- Marker board or flip chart, markers

HOW OFTEN SHOULD WE DO THIS TRAINING?

One time. It may be repeated if various leadership groups are to be addressed.

Training Step-by-Step

1. LEADER'S PREP

Study the Leader's Guide and view the **"For Board Members"** training track on the DVD. Be prepared to answer questions and address concerns.

2. GET STARTED

- Briefly explain the purpose of this session: to provide an overview of child sexual abuse in ministries, which is a critical issue facing faith communities.
- On the Training DVD go to **"Start Training Tracks."** Select **"For Board Members."**
- **View Video #1: "Child Protection as the Foundation of Your Ministry."**
- Pause at the end of Video #1 to discuss the following questions:

OPEN FOR DISCUSSION:

- The video acknowledges several objections ministry leaders and children's/youth workers have about introducing a child protection program. What issues does it raise in your mind regarding our ministry?

- Imagine that allegations of child sexual abuse were made against our ministry. What are some of the possible consequences we might face?

In the past, ministry board members have been found personally liable for cases of negligent screening and supervision when child sexual molestation occurred. It's important to remember that child protection programs not only safeguard children from being abused, but also provide solid protection for ministry leaders against being sued for negligence.

- What protection does our ministry have in place to safeguard board members from suffering the effects of a lawsuit? Are you willing to assume the legal risks if an incident of child sexual abuse should occur?

Child sexual abuse in faith communities is not just a financial issue. For every statistic about a claim that has been made, a real person has suffered untold trauma. The following segment may be difficult for some participants to watch. Sexual abuse has become an epidemic in our society, and likely there will be people on your governing board who have been victimized themselves. Be sensitive to the emotional reactions some participants may have, and adapt questions as needed.

- **View Video #2: "A Victim's Story."**

Wesley's story highlights several points:

- Child sexual abuse is a devastating experience for the victim.
- There are people in your ministry who have the potential to abuse children.
- Faith communities are vulnerable to child sexual abuse.

■ Ministries can re-victimize their members depending on how they respond to an allegation.

OPEN FOR DISCUSSION:

■ What effect did hearing Wesley's story have on you?

■ What do you believe children from the nursery to our high school youth group should expect from our ministry?

■ In what ways is our ministry vulnerable to child sexual abuse? How can these vulnerable areas be made more secure?

Sexual abuse is a complex issue, especially within faith communities. When trusted leaders and volunteers abuse their position of power with young people, the effects can be catastrophic. In this next video segment, you'll hear from a group of experts who deal with several different aspects of this problem. Their comments reveal the true cost—financial, emotional, spiritual, and physical—of a faith community becoming involved in an incident of child sexual abuse.

■ **View Video #3: "Sexual Abuse in Faith Communities: An Expert Roundtable." (15 minutes)**

OPEN FOR DISCUSSION

■ Do you believe the issue of sexual abuse has become a public health issue? If so, should the church lead the charge in eradicating it?

■ What would this look like for our faith community? What would this look like on a national level?

■ Is safety a core value of our children's ministry from infants to high schoolers? Which of our policies support this value?

■ As each expert points out, it's impossible to identify a potential sex offender relying on outward appearances and impressions alone. There are no distinguishing characteristics that identify someone as a predator. Knowing this, what are we doing to deter predators from gaining access to the children in our ministry?

Going Deeper ○ ○ ○ ○ ○ ○

What Is Child Sexual Abuse?

Part of supporting the development of a child protection program is understanding what child sexual abuse actually is. The precise legal definition of child sexual abuse or molestation varies from state to state, but it usually includes any form of sexual contact or exploitation in which a minor is being used for the sexual stimulation of the perpetrator. In a more general sense, child sexual abuse is:

Any sexual activity with a child whether in the home by a caretaker, in a day care situation, a foster/residential setting, or in any other setting, including on the street by a person unknown to the child. The abuser may be an adult, an adolescent, or another child, provided the child is four years older than the victim (National Resource Center on Child Sexual Abuse).

Child sexual abuse may be violent or non-violent, but all child sexual abuse is an exploitation of a child's vulnerability and powerlessness in which the abuser is fully responsible for the actions. Child sexual abuse is *criminal behavior* that involves children in sexual behaviors for which they are not personally, socially, and developmentally ready.

Child sexual abuse includes behaviors that involve aspects of both *touching* and *non-touching*.

Types of abuse that involve touching include:

- fondling
- oral, genital, and anal penetration

- intercourse
- forcible rape

Types of sexual abuse that do not involve touching include:

- verbal comments
- pornographic videos
- obscene phone calls
- exhibitionism
- allowing children to witness sexual activity

The full extent of child sexual abuse in our country is not known. Current conservative estimates suggest that between 500,000 and 1,500,000 children are sexually abused each year, although the actual number is likely to be higher because the greater percentage of these cases go unreported. A national retrospective study on the prevalence of child sexual abuse found that 27 percent of adult women and 16 percent of men claimed to have experienced some form of child sexual victimization. Over 25 percent indicated this occurred before the age of nine (Finkelhor, Hotaling, Lewis, and Smith, 1990).

Child sexual abuse occurs in all demographic, racial, ethnic, socio-economic, and religious groups. Strangers account for less than 20 percent of the abusers. Estimates indicate that when a known assailant commits the abuse, half of the time it is a father or stepfather, and the rest of the time it is a trusted adult who misuses his or her authority over children.

○   ○   ○

Some ministry leaders do not believe anyone in their ministry would harm a child. This is especially true among smaller faith communities where members are more likely to know one another. It's common for there to be a passive acceptance concerning the problem of child sexual abuse, but ministry leaders feel no need to address it at the congregational level. Our research indicates that smaller faith communities, especially those located in rural settings and small towns, are the least likely to screen volunteers.

In this next video, noted attorney Richard Hammar introduces the legal requirements every ministry must meet in order to provide a reasonable defense should they ever end up in court over the issue of child sexual abuse. Richard Hammar has spent the majority of his career creating resources to help keep children safe from sexual abuse, and to help ministries stay out of court over this highly litigated issue.

- **View Video #7: "Legal Requirements: The Church's Responsibility to Protect Kids (with Richard Hammar)."**

OPEN FOR DISCUSSION

- What about Richard Hammar's presentation made you feel nervous? What about it made you feel relieved?

- Given our current policies and practices relating to the screening, selection, and supervision of staff and volunteer workers, how would we hold up in a court of law if we were accused of hiring a predator?

- What action steps do we need to take to better safeguard our ministry and our most vulnerable members from ever being abused?

- What will we mandate to our ministry leaders in order to ensure that our ministry is a safe haven for children?

Going Deeper ○ ○ ○ ○ ○ ○

Why Ministries Are Susceptible to Predators

Ministries have unique features that can make them vulnerable to incidents of child molestation.

1. Trust. Ministries tend to be trusting and unsuspecting institutions. Even when questions are raised about a worker's conduct, leaders may ignore the evidence rather than question the worker's character or motives.

2. Need. Most ministries struggle to get adequate help for children and youth programs. Recruiting nursery workers, for example, can become an unending effort. Also, turnover among volunteer workers is high. Therefore, a willing volunteer worker provides welcome relief.

3. Lack of screening. Some ministries do nothing to screen youth workers. Complete strangers may be accepted to work with children without any investigation whatever.

4. Opportunity. Ministries provide ample opportunities for unsupervised personal contact between adults and children. This risk increases dramatically for overnight activities.

5. Access. The Boy Scouts, Big Brothers, and similar organizations have instituted comprehensive programs to reduce the risk of child molestation. Child molesters are attracted to institutions in which they have immediate access to potential victims in an atmosphere of complete trust—*the church*.

THE RESPONSE OF THE INSURANCE INDUSTRY

No one evaluates risk better than insurance companies. Some companies are reducing the coverage they provide for child abuse, and in some cases are excluding it entirely. Policies exclude damages based on intentional, criminal conduct.

▶*Action Item:*
Your governing board should immediately review your ministry's liability policy to determine whether you have any coverage for acts of molestation occurring on your property or during your activities, and if so, whether your coverage has been limited in any way.

Many ministries will discover that they either have no coverage for such incidents, or that the policy limits have been significantly reduced. If your ministry fits within either category, the procedures recommended in this book are of even greater relevance. Often, increased levels of coverage are available to faith communities and ministries that implement a prevention program.

THE LEGAL ENVIRONMENT

The number of lawsuits brought against faith communities as a result of child sexual abuse has risen substantially over the past several decades. Why the increase?

Media attention. The media has focused a lot of attention on child molestation cases—especially on those cases involving paid and volunteer workers. Often, front page publicity is given to these cases, and to the astronomical jury verdicts that are sometimes awarded.

Statute of limitations. Many states have greatly increased the period of time (the "statute of limitations") during which molestation victims must file a lawsuit. This has enabled victims to sue churches many years after an incident of molestation.

Theories of liability. Plaintiff attorneys have introduced innovative theories of liability that have assisted molestation victims in recovering financial damages.

Injury. The extent of the psychological and emotional injury experienced by victims of sexual molestation is real, and has only recently been fully appreciated.

Number of victims. Recent studies suggest that the number of adults who were sexually molested or abused as children is staggering. Some studies suggest that as many as 27 percent of adult females and 16 percent of adult males were victims of molestation as minors.

Reporting requirements. All 50 states require certain individuals ("mandatory reporters") to report known or reasonably suspected incidents of child abuse to state officials. This has exposed many cases of child abuse, and has made victims less willing to remain anonymous.

Support for litigation. An increasing number of attorneys and victim advocacy groups are encouraging sex-abuse victims to utilize litigation as a means to secure justice and promote personal healing.

WHY FAITH COMMUNITIES AND THEIR LEADERS ARE SUED

Most of the lawsuits filed against ministries for acts of child molestation have alleged that the faith community was legally accountable either on the basis of *negligent hiring* or *negligent supervision*. Both theories of liability are pivotal issues. The term *negligence* means recklessness.

Negligent hiring simply means that the ministry failed to act responsibly and with due care in the selection of workers (both volunteer and compensated) for positions involving the supervision or custody of minors. A church may exercise sufficient care in the hiring of an individual, but still be legally accountable for acts of molestation on the basis of negligent supervision. Negligent supervision means that a ministry did not exercise sufficient care in supervising a worker.

Ministry leaders need to understand the extent of their liability. Faith communities are not "guarantors" of the safety and well being of children. They are not absolutely liable for every injury that occurs on their premises or in the course of their activities. Generally, they are responsible only for those injuries that result from their negligence.

Assume that an incident of abuse occurs in your faith community, and that the pastor is asked to testify during the trial. The victim's lawyer asks, "What did you or your staff do to prevent this tragedy from occurring? What procedures did you utilize to check the molester's background and supervise his work with children?" What would your pastor say? If the answer is "nothing," you can well imagine the jury's reaction. The only question in the jurors' minds at this point is the size of the verdict.

○   ○   ○

IS SCREENING TOO BURDENSOME?

Some ministry leaders don't screen workers because they find it too burdensome. They don't like the time and expense associated with screening. If this is the case in your ministry, consider the following:

- American society will not excuse faith communities from the protection of children. Faith communities are now being held accountable by the media, by their own members, and by society at large. The safety of children outweighs any other consideration, and no jury will tolerate any excuse for its absence—especially one stating that "screening is inconvenient."

- Your liability insurance policy may exclude or limit coverage for acts of child molestation. If so, your ministry is faced with a potentially enormous uninsured risk. Reducing this risk is worth whatever inconvenience might be generated in implementing a screening procedure. Just ask any member of a ministry in which such an incident has occurred.

- In some cases, ministry board members may be held personally liable for acts of child molestation if gross negligence is found. The efficacy of the ministry's screening process will be one factor in that determination.

3. WHAT'S NEXT?

After everyone's had a chance to ask final questions or offer comments, propose to your board to move forward on this issue. With their support, request that they create (or allow you to create) a child protection team. This team will be responsible for drafting ministry policies regarding protecting kids at ministry and for initiating training for ministry leaders. You can show them the sample Child Protection Plan we've provided in Appendix 1 at the back of this book, and ask for their support in customizing a plan for your ministry. From there, the child protection team will be responsible for training Ministry Leaders on new policies and procedures. Ministry Leaders will then train all staff and volunteers who work with minors, and they will also be responsible for screening, selecting, and supervising workers according to these new procedures.

Chapter Three

Training Ministry Leaders

PREPARING YOUR TRAINERS

Making safety your top priority.

Let the little children come to me, and do not hinder them, for the kingdom of God belongs to such as these. (Luke 18:16)

Ministry Leaders will be the key people in charge of training staff and volunteer workers in child protection. This chapter is written for those who will be training Ministry Leaders on child protection, such as Child Advocates or a Safety Team Leader. If these roles do not exist, Ministry Leaders should train themselves using this chapter as well as all other chapters in this book. On the DVD, choose the training track **"For Child Advocates and Ministry Leaders."**

Ministry Leaders will be the foot soldiers in implementing a child protection program. They will be the ones who will explain and enforce screening and supervision policies and procedures with other staff and children's/youth workers. To effectively do this, they must fully understand the purpose of the program and personally endorse its goals.

Some Ministry Leaders may resist a child protection program. They may see it as intrusive and adding to their work, or complicating their efforts at staffing and managing programs for young people. We'll address objections like these in this training. Our goal is to help create a safe environment for effective ministry. The only way to accomplish this is to make your child protection program doable. The step-by-step training that follows will equip Ministry Leaders for immediate action. Let's go!

Training Overview

For Ministry Leaders (approximately 4 hours)

Items that are marked with a dashed line and arrow along the side indicate content that is also provided in the Trainee Workbook. This will help you know which material students are viewing and what is reserved just for your Leader's Guide. Answers are also provided for fill in the blank sections.

WHAT'S THE GOAL OF THIS TRAINING?

- To increase awareness of the symptoms and consequences of child sexual abuse.

- To underscore the ministry's vulnerability to child sexual abuse.

- To create an understanding of liability concerns and ministry policy guidelines pertaining to screening, supervision, and reporting.

- To provide instruction on worker selection and worker training.

WHO SHOULD ATTEND?

- All paid or volunteer ministry leaders who oversee children or youth activities, including the following:
- Nursery supervisor
- Day care director
- Leader of club programs
- Youth ministers and sponsors
- Sunday School superintendents and departmental leaders
- VBS director
- Children's choral director
- Christian school principals
- Other ministry leaders working with children or youth

WHAT RESOURCES FROM MY REDUCING THE RISK KIT WILL I NEED?

- *Reducing the Risk* Training DVD

- Copies of church policies
- *Reducing the Risk* Screening Forms & Records File for Volunteers
- *Reducing the Risk* Trainee Workbook and pen for each student

WHAT ADDITIONAL SUPPLIES DO I NEED TO LEAD THE TRAINING?

- DVD player and monitor
- Marker board or flip chart, markers

HOW OFTEN SHOULD THIS TRAINING BE OFFERED?

- Training should be offered as part of orientation for all new leaders who have contact with children. Ministry Leaders should repeat child protection training on a periodic basis.

Training Step-By-Step

1. LEADER'S PREP

All participants should be given a copy of the Trainee Workbook. If you are training more than six people, you may want to break into smaller groups of three to four people to discuss questions after each video segment.

2. GET STARTED

- Introduce yourself briefly. Instruct participants to follow along with their Trainee Workbook so they can jot down notes while watching the video segments.

- On the Training DVD go to **"Start Training Tracks."** Select **"For Child Advocates and Ministry Leaders."**

- **View Video #1: "Child Protection as the Foundation of Your Ministry."**

OPEN FOR DISCUSSION

- What led you to serve in your area of ministry?

- Effective ministry can only take place if a child feels safe. How safe do you think kids feel when they come to Sunday school or other ministry programs? What does your ministry do to ensure children's safety?

- In the opening video, the children's leader checked in each child by giving them a special bracelet to identify them. What check-in procedure does your ministry use to ensure kids leave with the correct adult?

- Did you resonate with any of the objections to implementing a child protection program that you heard in the opening video? Could you envision others in your ministry voicing these or other objections?

A prevention program can reduce risk through relatively simple procedures. However, be prepared to respond to the following concerns:

"The risk of this happening in our ministry is small."

Response. Focus on the legal and moral obligations of the ministry. Are those leaders raising this concern willing to assume the legal risks if an incident should occur? If an incident occurs, issues of negligent selection and negligent supervision will focus directly upon the actions and guidance of the ministry leaders.

"Screening will turn people off from serving."

Response. Community standards are changing. All organizations that work with children are implementing screening procedures. Workers understand that screening is required in many different settings, and parents want to know that their children are safe. Proper implementation and communication provide the answer to this concern. The focus should be upon providing a safe place for youth and children. Faith community members will rally around that objective.

"This violates our trust in one another."

Response. Just the opposite is occurring. As members recognize that their faith community cares deeply about the welfare of the youth and children, their trust in ministry programs and their appreciation for the ministry's leadership will increase. They can have confidence that their faith community provides a safe and secure environment for youth and children. In whose custody would you prefer your children to be—a ministry with an established and caring prevention program, or one where anyone can have access to your children? The key to promoting trust is how the program is implemented and communicated to the faith community.

Fill in the blanks:

When it comes to (child sexual abuse), many people still don't believe that the (danger) is real.

When a child has a good ministry experience, they're more likely to (grow) in their faith and stay involved with the (church/ministry). When a child is a victim of sexual abuse in a faith community, the (effects) are devastating and last the child's (lifetime).

You will be viewing a story of a youth who was victimized by his youth pastor. As you'll see, one case of abuse can have an incredible impact on individuals, their families, and the faith community.

- **View Video #2: "A Victim's Story."** *(This video may be difficult for some people to watch. Although this segment is not graphic in its description of sexual abuse, it may elicit strong emotions if you have experienced abuse or you know loved ones who have endured this trauma.)*

OPEN FOR DISCUSSION:

- At the beginning of Wesley's story, what were some signs of a healthy relationship between a student and his youth pastor? What were clues that the relationship was not healthy?

- In your ministry, what do you do to monitor and hold staff and workers accountable for their behavior?

- Teens are highly susceptible to sexual abuse. Ministries tend to loosen their safety policies as kids get older, mistakenly believing kids will be able to discern dangerous individuals or situations. What's your reaction to Wesley's story? What responsibility do you think the church had to him and his family?

- How do you think Wesley's family felt when no one at their church believed their allegations? *(You'll learn more about how to respond to an allegation later in this training.)*

If teens are vulnerable to predators, how much more so young children! It's up to adults to provide protective boundaries to keep minors from being exposed to harmful individuals.

Fill in the blanks:

For Wesley, child sexual abuse (<u>destroyed</u>) his relationship with (<u>God</u>). Wesley's story is tragic, but it shares a common thread that links him to other victims: You cannot tell who is or who isn't a (<u>sex offender</u>).

Although Wesley was an older teen when his abuse occurred, as a (<u>minor</u>), it was not his responsibility to (<u>protect</u>) himself. Children, whether they are 7 or 17, are not expected to use perfect (<u>judgment</u>). This is one of the main reasons our legal system entrusts children to (<u>our</u>) care.

Going Deeper ○ ○ ○ ○ ○

Consequences of Child Sexual Abuse

Child sexual abuse robs children of their childhood and can potentially scar its young victims for life. Too often in the past, the effects of abuse were minimized or dismissed. Children were viewed as being resilient. But recent research has shown that children can suffer significant pain from even a single abusive incident. Faith communities must be aware of the pain and long-term suffering that can accompany such abuse. Abused children can display a wide range of negative symptoms in the aftermath of abuse, including abnormal fears, post-traumatic stress disorder (PTSD), aggressive behavior, sexual acting out, depression, diffused sexual identity, and poor self-esteem (Kendall-Tackett, Williams, and Finkelhor, 1991). The incidence of sexually transmitted disease is also a possible outcome.

The degree of damage depends upon several factors, including the intensity, duration, and frequency of the abuse. In addition, the *relationship* of the perpetrator to the child matters. If the abuser is a known and trusted authority figure in the child's life, the degree of impact increases dramatically.

Consequences of child sexual abuse can plague victims into adulthood. Outcome studies of adult survivors of child sexual abuse suggest the following effects: sexual dysfunction, eating disorders, substance abuse, promiscuity, disassociation from emotions, and possible perpetration of sexual abuse on others (Geffner, 1992).

As we saw in Video #2, **"A Victim's Story,"** when ministry leaders, pastors, and respected volunteers perpetrate the abuse, lifelong religious confusion and deep feelings of enmity toward God and the church can also occur.

○   ○   ○

■ **View Video #3: "Sexual Abuse in Faith Communities— An Expert Roundtable"**

This DVD features five experts who deal with different aspects of sexual abuse in faith communities. You'll hear from a risk manager who helps develop safety resources for churches and faith-based programs, a staff psychologist who helped create his church's child protection program, an insurance claims manager who understands the legal impact of sexual abuse allegations, a clinical psychologist who specializes in counseling victims of sexual abuse, and an insurance industry leader who works among faith communities of every denomination.

OPEN FOR DISCUSSION:

- Do you think faith communities are more at risk for being sued today than they were 20 years ago? Why or why not?
- What are the factors that make faith communities and ministries particularly vulnerable?
- If you were to put on an "offender eye," what area of ministry might be vulnerable?
- Which vulnerabilities are easiest to correct? Which would be most difficult to correct?
- If you can't identify a sex offender based on outward appearances and impressions, what can you do to protect children from being victims?

Going Deeper ◦ ◦ ◦ ◦ ◦

What Is Child Sexual Abuse?

Part of supporting the creation of a child protection program is understanding what child sexual abuse actually is. The precise legal definition of child sexual abuse or molestation varies from state to state, but it usually includes any form of sexual contact or exploitation in which a minor is being used for the sexual stimulation of the perpetrator. In a more general sense, child sexual abuse is:

Any sexual activity with a child whether in the home by a caretaker, in a day care situation, a foster/residential setting, or in any other setting, including on the street by a person unknown to the child. The abuser may be an adult, an adolescent, or another child, provided the child is four years older than the victim (National Resource Center on Child Sexual Abuse).

Child sexual abuse may be violent or non-violent, but all child sexual abuse is an exploitation of a child's vulnerability and powerlessness in which the abuser is fully responsible for the actions. Child sexual abuse is *criminal behavior* that involves children in sexual behaviors for which they are not personally, socially, and developmentally ready.

Child sexual abuse includes behaviors that involve aspects of both *touching* and *non-touching*.

Types of abuse that involve touching include:

- fondling
- oral, genital, and anal penetration
- intercourse
- forcible rape

Types of sexual abuse that do not involve touching include:

- verbal comments
- pornographic videos
- obscene phone calls
- exhibitionism
- allowing children to witness sexual activity

The full extent of child sexual abuse in our country is not known. Conservative estimates suggest that between 500,000 and 1,500,000 children are sexually abused each year, although actual the number is likely to be higher because the greater percentage of these cases go unreported. A national retrospective study on the prevalence of child sexual abuse found that 27 percent of adult women and 16 percent of men claimed to have experienced some form of child sexual victimization. Over 25 percent indicated this occurred before the age of nine (Finkelhor, Hotaling, Lewis, and Smith, 1990).

Child sexual abuse occurs in all demographic, racial, ethnic, socio-economic, and religious groups. Strangers account for less than 20 percent of the abusers. Estimates indicate that when a known assailant

○   ○   ○

commits the abuse, half of the time it is a father or stepfather, and the rest of the time it is a trusted adult who misuses his or her authority over children.

Going Deeper ○ ○ ○ ○ ○ ○

Symptoms of Molestation

Ministry workers and staff members should be alert to the physical signs of abuse and molestation, as well as to the behavioral and verbal signs a victim may exhibit. Some of the more common signs are summarized below.

Physical signs may include:

- lacerations and bruises
- nightmares
- irritation, pain, or injury to the genital area
- difficulty with urination
- discomfort when sitting
- torn or bloody underclothing
- venereal disease

Behavioral signs may include:

- anxiety when approaching the ministry
- nervous or hostile behavior toward adults
- sexual self-consciousness
- "acting out" of sexual behavior
- withdrawal from ministry activities and friends

Verbal signs may include the following statements:

- "I don't like [a particular ministry worker]."
- "[A ministry worker] does things to me when we're alone."

- "I don't like to be alone with [a ministry worker]."

- "[A ministry worker] fooled around with me."

(Sloan, 1983)

⊙   ⊙   ⊙

In **"Testimony of a Sex Offender,"** the former convicted pedophile says, "No one plans to become a sex offender." So how does this crime happen? As you'll hear in this video segment, it can evolve out of learned behavior—abuse experienced by the predator at an early age, which is then fostered by repeated exposure to pornography. Understanding the mindset of a predator doesn't excuse the crime. But knowing the elements that are commonly present in predators' backgrounds gives us insight into the very real danger of pornography and the insidious impact it can have on individuals and their behavior.

- **View Video #4: "Testimony of a Sex Offender."** *(Similar to "A Victim's Story," This may be difficult for some participants to watch. Let participants know that although this segment is not graphic in its description of sexual abuse, it may elicit strong emotions in those who have experienced abuse or known loved ones who have endured this trauma.)*

OPEN FOR DISCUSSION:

- What thoughts and emotions surfaced when you listened to the offender's story?

- Although we never saw the former perpetrator's full image, if you passed him on the street, you would probably never guess that he had committed this crime. Knowing this, what can a ministry do to avoid inadvertently recruiting dangerous workers?

- How equipped do you feel to adequately perform a thorough screening process?

⊙   ⊙   ⊙

> **Tip** The Screening Forms & Records File for Volunteers provides a turn-key way for you to begin to screen volunteers who will work with minors. For clergy and employees, visit *YourChurchResources.com* for employment screening forms and applications.

Going Deeper ○ ○ ○ ○ ○ ○

Ward Off the Opportunists;
Eliminate the Opportunities!

You can learn more about the behavioral profile of a sex offender and find more tools for dealing with sex offenders who are part of your faith community at **ReducingTheRisk.com**. As a ministry leader, your job is not to guess whether a person is a molester or not. Your focus should be on properly screening *all* candidates, because you cannot tell who is or is not a sex offender.

In addition, solid supervision practices will provide your second layer of defense to deter predators from working in your ministry. Put another way, your job is to *ward off the opportunists and eliminate the opportunities!*

Religious Conversion

Should religious conversion make a difference in working with children or youth for individuals who have been guilty of child molestation in the past? Occasionally, such persons freely admit to a prior incident, but now insist that as a result of their conversion experience, they no longer present any risk to children. These individuals should not be allowed to serve in any position with children or youth. The issue is not the person's conversion or salvation, but the safety of the children and the responsibility of ministry leaders. Establishing safe practices for workers is consistent with biblical teaching. The faith community's most important duty is to safeguard children.

Furthermore, from a legal standpoint, a ministry that permits such an individual to work with children or youth—solely on the basis of the professed religious conversion—will have a virtually indefensible position should another incident of molestation occur. These cases can lead to punitive damages for the ministry and personal liability for its leaders.

Fill in the blanks:

Child sexual abuse is not (<u>denominational</u>).

Child sexual abuse do not only affects churches (<u>financially</u>). It also destroys (<u>credibility</u>) and people's (<u>trust</u>) in the Church.

Offenders look for (<u>child-nurturing</u>) environments, and churches are child-nurturing.

Predators (<u>groom</u>) children as well as the adult community.

The two-adult rule is for the safety of children and for the protection of (<u>adults</u>) against (<u>false allegations</u>).

In Video #5, noted attorney Richard Hammar makes his case for why screening is critical in safeguarding children from predators. He provides a five-step plan as the basis for your child protection program. Get your pen and workbook ready—you'll want to take notes!

- **View Video #5: "Screening & Selection: Your First Line of Defense" (with Richard Hammar).**

- **View Video #6: "Screening & Selection: The Candidate (a short film)"**

OPEN FOR DISCUSSION:

- How would you describe the ideal candidate for working with children or youth in your ministry? What characteristics would you want? What would you definitely try to avoid?

- Your role as a leader is not to identify molesters, but rather to eliminate the opportunity for molesters to gain access to kids. How well do our current screening and supervision practices deter sex offenders from trying to serve in your ministries?

- What are Richard Hammar's five steps for a successful child protection program? Which of these five steps are you already doing?

- Would a jury be convinced that your ministry is using reasonable care in the way you select ministry workers if they scrutinized your hiring practices?

Pass out copies of *Reducing the Risk* **Screening Forms & Records File for Volunteers**. Explain the screening procedures your ministry has adopted (or is developing), for screening and selecting volunteer workers, which may include:

- screening procedures
- screening forms
- requirements for workers
- interviewing
- reference checks
- criminal records checks

Ministry leaders need to clearly understand each of the components of the screening process. They may have a number of procedural and logistical questions about these policies, including how they should be implemented in their particular situations. To save time, you may need to meet with some leaders on an individual basis to discuss their concerns.

▶ *Action Item:*

Reinforce the rationale for these procedures. Keep the focus on providing a safe environment for the children and for children's/youth workers.

Point out that your ministry has adopted some or all of the policies and procedures mentioned in the video to reduce the risk of child sexual abuse. (Hand out copies of your church's proposed or adopted child protection plan.) These safeguards address four main areas that pertain to child safety in your programs.

- Worker selection
- Worker supervision

- Reporting an allegation
- Responding to an allegation

Now that you've had a chance to review your church's child protection plan, look more closely at the steps your ministry will take to properly screen potential children's/youth volunteers. Open a copy of the **Screening Forms & Records File for Volunteers**.

Just as a hurdle is an obstacle to a runner, slowing them down, ministries create procedures that present a barrier to potential molesters. The more safeguards that are in place, the lower the risk of possible abuse in our faith community. Here's how ministries reduce opportunities for potential molesters:

1. Application Form

Requiring a written application for volunteers serves the same role as it does for paid employees. The goal is to document the selection process, and to be able to demonstrate that the ministry meets the test of reasonable care. Remember, the focus is not upon the employment status of the worker, but on the worker's responsibilities. A ministry can be just as liable for the negligent selection of a volunteer as it can be for a paid employee. Use the Screening Forms & Records File for Volunteers, and visit **YourChurchResources.com** for employment applications and screening forms for paid staff and clergy.

2. Reference check forms

Ministries conduct reference checks of all individuals, former employers, and organizations listed in the application. It is critical that the applicant sign a liability release before the reference checks are done. This provides authorization to conduct reference checks, and releases references to respond to the request for information. The release should permit you to interview anyone you believe can provide helpful information.

What should you do if a listed reference or former employer refuses to respond? Some organizations refuse to hire a prospective employee in this situation because the failure to respond raises a red flag that requires further exploration. A simple explanation may exist, but in some cases, the reference may not want to share information for fear of being sued.

In certain situations, the concept of "qualified privilege" may also become relevant. Many states recognize a "qualified privilege" on the part of employers to share information about former employees with other employers. This ordinarily means that such statements cannot be the basis for defamation unless they are made with "malice." In this context, malice means either that the former employer knew that the statements made were false, or that statements were made with a reckless disregard as to their truth or falsity. In other words, so long as the reference has a reasonable basis for the statements made about a former worker, the remarks will be protected in many states by a qualified privilege. A local attorney can advise whether or not your state recognizes a qualified privilege under such circumstances.

Important: *If you are listed as a reference, and have negative information that you feel compelled to share, make sure that the applicant has signed a liability release. Also, determine whether a qualified privilege exists.*

3. Personal interview

A personal interview is an excellent way to gauge a candidate's character and explore their qualifications directly. Information obtained in the reference checks may provide assistance in formulating the interview questions. In addition, other organizations—such as state agencies responsible for investigating reports of child abuse, the school district, Big Brothers, Big Sisters, the Boy Scouts, Girl Scouts, Boys Clubs, Girls Clubs, and the local YMCA or YWCA—may also have materials that can be used to assist staff members who will conduct interviews. Employees of these agencies may be able to provide helpful assistance regarding their own screening process and interview questions.

4. Additional background checks

No court, in any reported decision, has found a church liable on the basis of negligent selection for the molestation of a child on the ground that the church failed to conduct a criminal records check on the molester before using him to work with children. That said, churches that conduct criminal records checks on volunteers who work with minors will be in a better position to defend against an allegation of negligent selection than those who do not conduct such checks. It is worth noting that a growing number of youth-serving organizations are performing criminal records checks on volunteers, and this suggests that the court one day may conclude that "reasonable care" in the selection of children's/youth volunteers necessitates criminal records checks.

Today, such checks can be conducted online. For more information visit **ReducingTheRisk.com**. While a quick check on **nsopr.gov** (National Sex Offender Public Registry) may only take a couple of minutes to receive results, other background searches take longer. There are a variety of criminal records checks available to ministry leaders for screening employees and volunteer workers. These include county, state, and national checks. On their own, no one search provides a complete picture of a person's past. Plus, if you don't know the rules governing which reports you are allowed to use to make a hiring decision, as outlined in the Fair Credit Reporting Act, you can easily misinterpret and misuse the information. We recommend using a reputable background check service provider who can access a full search and interpret the data for you.

The topic of background checks continues to be an area of confusion for many ministries. ReducingTheRisk.com provides information to clarify this complex topic and to help you find a reputable background check provider.

Going Deeper ○ ○ ○ ○ ○ ○

Megan's Laws

The Supreme Court's decision to uphold the constitutionality of state "Megan's Laws" gives youth-serving organizations the ability to perform checks of national and state sex offense registries, such as **nsopr.gov**, without the knowledge or consent of the individual they are checking. As a result, an increasing number of ministries are checking their state sex offender registry for anyone who will have access to minors.

But ministry leaders should be aware of four limitations associated with these checks:

1. Sex offender registries only include convictions for specified sex crimes. Other crimes (kidnapping, murder, assault, etc.) are also relevant in making a decision regarding the suitability of a person to have access to minors.

2. Sex offender registries only contain criminal convictions after a specified date (which in many states is fairly recent).

3. Sex offender registries only include criminal records in one state.

4. Sex offender registries are not easily accessible by the public in some states. For example, in some states the sex offender registry is maintained by law enforcement agencies, and the public can review the registry only by contacting such an agency.

As a result, ministry leaders should not view a sex offender registry check as the *only* screening procedure that is necessary. At best, it is one component in an overall screening strategy that includes an application, interview, reference checks, and possibly other criminal records checks.

> **Tip** If you do a sex offender registry search, be sure to retain a copy of the results, even if a person's name is not listed on the registry. This will document that you performed a search, which will be relevant evidence in the event that your church is later sued on the basis of negligent selection for the molestation of a child by that person.

What do you do if you discover that your state sex offender registry contains the name of an applicant for youth ministry? First, you need to be absolutely sure that the registry identified the same person as the one you were investigating. In some cases, the registry will contain other identifying information (address, phone number, etc.) that will confirm a person's identity. If not, then call the telephone number listed on the registry website and ask for additional information.

You can quickly find links to the Megan's Law sex offender registries of all 50 states at **Klaaskids.org**. Just click on your state and you will be directed to information that is specific to your state, including the name and telephone number of a contact person you can call with any questions; a summary of the kinds of sex offenders who are required to register; and a link to search the registry via the internet (if available).

- **View Video #7: "Legal Requirements: The Church's Responsibility to Protect Kids."**

▶ Tip In this DVD segment, Richard Hammar acknowledges that institutions, such as our public school system, interpret the two-adult rule to mean that as long as there is more than one child present, it is acceptable to have only one adult supervising. However, no adult should ever be alone with one child. Some insurance companies and major youth-serving ministries strongly prefer having at least two non-related adults present in all situations. When you establish your ministry's interpretation of the two-adult rule, be sure to enforce it consistently. As Richard Hammar points out, the worst position for a ministry to be in is to have a policy and fail to enforce it consistently.

OPEN FOR DISCUSSION:

- What is your ministry's policy on adult-child supervision?
- Child protection policies should be designed first and foremost with children's safety in mind, not for the convenience of the adults in ministry. Is this true of the policies in your children's ministry?

Fill in the blanks:

- The (<u>public</u>) will no longer accept the a faith community's excuse to do (<u>nothing</u>) to protect children.

- NSOPR.gov lists known (<u>sex offenders</u>). This is one fast, free online tool, but it is only one of many components that should go into a thorough (<u>background</u>) check.

- **View Video #8: "Supervising Scenarios: What Would You Do?"** In this fast-paced motion graphics segment, leaders will have a chance to view several challenging ministry moments. Shout out solutions. But you'll need to think fast—you only get about 30 seconds (usually the amount of time you'll have in real life) to solve each dilemma.

  Note to Leader: *Plan on pausing the video after each scenario is finished to give your group time to discuss alternative solutions.*

OPEN FOR DISCUSSION:

- Which scenario did you find the most difficult to solve?

- What real-world challenges might make it tough for you or your ministry workers to comply with supervision polices?

- What are the high-risk areas and activities of your ministry?

▶ **Tip** A youth worker is anyone under age 18 who is volunteering in the children's or youth ministry. Because of their age, they do not qualify as an adult in the two-adult rule.

○　○　○

Going Deeper ○ ○ ○ ○ ○ ○

How Risky Is a Situation?

Not all activities bear the same level of risk. As a result, the level of supervision should correspond to the level of risk. General supervision is appropriate for low-risk activities. But as the risk increases, supervision should increase as well.

What is it that makes some activities higher risk than others? For example, in general we can say that a "lock-in" represents a higher level of risk than a Sunday school class. But what is it that makes the lock-in a higher risk activity? The answer lies in three factors: isolation, accountability, and power.

The safest environment is one with low isolation, high accountability, and a balance of power. Molesters, on the other hand, look for programs with increased isolation, lower accountability, and opportunities to maintain power over their victims.

By analyzing the degree of isolation, accountability, and power in any given situation, you can quickly adjust your supervision level to lower the level of risk for something going wrong.

Risk Factor 1: Isolation

Risk increases as isolation increases.

Most, but not all, sexual abuse occurs in isolated settings. Four factors affect isolation: (1) the number of people present, (2) the time of the activity, (3) the location of the activity, and (4) the physical arrangements.

Let's practice applying these principles:

> **Example:** *Two adults and one youth worker are serving in the nursery during the 9 a.m. service. Two babies are asleep in cribs, and four infants are laying on baby play mats while the workers sit next to them on the floor. One baby wakes up and needs a diaper change, so one adult volunteer brings her to the changing table in the far corner of the room. The second baby wakes up and begins to cry, so the other adult picks up this baby to comfort her and walks out of*

the room to avoid setting off a chain reaction of crying babies. That
leaves the 13-year-old youth worker watching four babies.

In this example, isolation is low initially. The nursery is well-supervised—until the two adults get called away to tend to the babies. At this point, the nursery now poses a higher level of risk for the infants and the workers. The youth worker is too distracted trying to monitor the four babies she is now in charge of that she fails to notice the woman changing the baby's diaper in the corner. Diapering—or any other bathroom-related issues—should never be done in isolation. It leaves the child dangerously vulnerable, plus it puts the ministry worker in a position where no one can vouch for her actions. Also, with a 13-year-old youth worker and an adult worker, there is a disparity of age between volunteers. It is highly unlikely that the student worker will speak up if something seems out of place with her superior, let alone know to hold her supervisor accountable for her actions. And finally, while the likelihood of a woman being a sex offender is low (studies estimate that approximately 94 percent of all perpetrators of sexual abuse are male), it does occur. Steer clear of making supervision policies based on the gender of workers. And remember, you can't tell by looking at someone whether he or she is a sex offender.

A safer solution for this nursery example would have been for the woman with the crying baby to call for back-up and request that another adult step in until she can calm the crying baby. Or she could have remained just outside the door where she could monitor the youth worker and the woman changing the diaper until she was finished. The goal should always be to create settings where isolation is eliminated and accountability exists.

Example: *Teachers invite their Sunday morning class to return to the church on Sunday afternoon at 3 p.m. for a party. No other activities are present on church property at that time.*

In this example, the children meet in the same location in the afternoon as they did in the morning. The change in time, however, alters the number of people present in the building. As a result, the risk environment has changed. Isolation has increased, so risk has also increased. This means the supervision should also increase and become more accountable—having at least two non-related adults present, for example, as well as having approval to sponsor the activity.

Let's look at another variation of this example. What if the party occurs at a local restaurant rather than at the church? The typical restaurant does not represent isolated space. However, other risks are present, including transportation to and from the restaurant. In addition, other safety factors require the need for two or more adults for any activity that is held off of church property. If one adult becomes unavailable for any reason, a second adult will be needed.

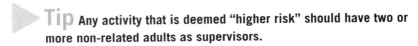 **Tip** **Any activity that is deemed "higher risk" should have two or more non-related adults as supervisors.**

Risk Factor 2: Accountability

Risk increases as accountability decreases.

The sexual abuse of children always occurs in settings without proper accountability. Notice the relationship between risk and accountability in each of the following examples.

—**Fred,** *a college student and a volunteer worker with the church's high school youth group, announces he is available for transportation if any of the members need a ride to group activities. Anne, a 17-year-old high school senior, asks Fred for a ride.*

—**Stan,** *the new youth pastor, wants to meet with members of the youth group to get to know them better. He decides to pick up students after school and take them out to get some ice cream. However, church policy requires that he must obtain permission in advance for such meetings. The pastor decides that another youth supervisor must be present.*

—**Randy,** *an adult member of First Church, volunteers to pick up a 10-year-old boy on his way to church each week. The boy lives with his mother, who is delighted to have a "father figure" express an interest in her son.*

In the three examples above, only the middle one demonstrates the use of accountability. Accountability involves justifying one's actions. Since sexual molestation cannot be justified, the perpetrators of abuse avoid settings in which they must give an account of their behavior. That's why they seek isolated settings, act in secrecy, and attempt to maintain power and control over their victims. Also, some workers, although they have had no prior intent on engaging in misconduct, may nevertheless cross a boundary under certain circumstances. Supervision policies that require accountability help reduce opportunities for exploiting kids. Three factors affect the accountability of supervisors in ministry programs involving children: (1) the personal character and integrity of the adult worker, (2) the number of people present for the activity, and (3) the degree of openness and approval associated with the activity.

Let's take a closer look at each factor.

1. Personal character and integrity. Clearly, a person's character and integrity affect risk, and that is why screening workers is a vital part of a prevention program. Parents assume that their children will be safe when they leave them in the care of another adult. Embedded in that assumption is that the supervising adult is trustworthy and has the best interests of the children at heart. Unfortunately, as the events of recent years have demonstrated, that assumption is not always true. As a result, reasonable care means that individuals who work with children need to be screened. The goal is to gain assurance that individuals have been accountable in the past and are likely to be accountable in the future.

2. The number of people present. As a general rule: the more adults, the better. Accountability increases when two or more non-related adults are present for activities that involve children and youth. Having multiple adults present decreases the risk of isolation and helps to maintain a better balance of power and control.

It is also a good idea to use a "building monitor" to inspect vacant rooms, buildings that are set apart, and private areas such as restrooms. People are less likely to engage in inappropriate conduct if they think someone is watching.

3. Degree of openness and approval. Openness is also important for accountability to occur. Ministry leaders should be fully aware of all activities in advance, and approve the content, activities, and leadership of each program. Individuals acting in secrecy raise immediate red flags. All activities sponsored by the ministry or that take place on ministry property should require advance approval. Other factors such as lighting, windows, open doors, and the use of video surveillance equipment can enhance the level of openness and reduce secrecy of activities that occur on ministry property.

Let's now use the risk factors of isolation and accountability to analyze the following example.

> **Example:** *A fourth grade Sunday school class has two non-related adult teachers. The class meets at the home of one of the teachers on a Friday night from 7-9 p.m. to play volleyball. Both teachers are present, and parents are also invited to attend. The Christian Education Director has approved the activity. Both teachers went through a screening program before they began working with children.*

The first point to notice is the event is being held off of church property, which makes it higher risk. This triggers the need for two or more non-related adults, such as the two teachers. Parents are also invited to attend, which further lowers isolation and increases accountability. Risk decreases even further since both teachers have gone through a screening process.

In this example, the risk of abuse is relatively low, yet other factors can contribute to a dynamic risk environment, which can change at any moment. Imagine, for example, that one child gets another child alone in a bedroom while everyone else plays outside. Abuse could occur in that isolated setting. To avoid such a scenario, boundaries should be established concerning the use of the house. Furthermore, those responsible for supervision should be aware of such concerns and take appropriate actions to monitor the space and maintain an open environment that facilitates low risk.

Next, let's create a few variations in this example to show how easily the risk environment can be altered. First, suppose parents are not invited. Second, only one teacher is present. Third, no one on the church staff knows about the event. Fourth, no screening occurred, and the teacher has a criminal record that no one knows about. Fifth, the time is extended to 11 p.m. Sixth, only boys are invited, and the event includes a sleepover. Each of these factors increases the level of risk as isolation is increased and accountability is decreased.

Let's now look at the third risk factor—the level of power that exists.

Risk Factor 3: Power

Risk increases when there is an imbalance of power, authority, influence, and control between a potential abuser and a potential victim.

One reason that children are so vulnerable to sexual predators is the imbalance of power related to age, size, strength, and also control and authority. Most child victims of sexual abuse know and trust their abuser. They may also fear the person. Once abuse occurs, perpetrators will use their power, authority, and influence to promote silence.

Control can be exerted in many ways, both physically and psychologically. Some abusers use "grooming" techniques to gain the trust and control of a child. They may offer cash, gifts, trips, fun experiences, and shower the child with attention and favors. They may also use blackmail, threats, physical force, and intimidation. In addition, predatory abusers often select their victims carefully to increase their likelihood of success. Children who are targets for abuse are no match for such predators.

What makes the problem unusually difficult in ministry settings is that the abuser is often a respected member of the faith community.

Often, these individuals will also use their spiritual authority as a means of power and control. Ministry leaders and parents are sometimes slow to see the signs of abuse because they, too, may trust and respect the abuser.

Abuse is less likely to occur when a balance of power exists. A growing number of ministry-related abuse cases involve another child as the perpetrator of the abuse. In part, these cases occur because of an imbalance of power, which is typically age-related. It is less common, for example, for a 9-year-old to molest another 9-year-old than for a 15-year-old to molest a 7-year-old.

MINISTRY ACTIVITIES

By their very nature, some activities represent a higher level of risk for sexual molestation than do others. These activities often increase isolation and lower accountability. Ministry leaders should pay careful attention to and increase supervision for the following events:

- Any activity that occurs in a home
- Any overnight activity, including lock-ins, camping trips, or staying in a hotel
- Any activity that involves changing clothes or becoming undressed, such as in locker rooms or dressing rooms
- Any activity that involves groups of children with age differences of four years or more
- Any activity that occurs in a natural, isolated environment, such as a building that is set off by itself, or a park that has secluded areas

Consider the following two scenarios in light of the three risk factors of isolation, accountability, and power.

Scenario 1: *The youth pastor picks up one or more youth members in his car. Sometimes the meetings are directly after school, other times they are at night or on a weekend. Many of the meetings are at the youth pastor's apartment. Sometimes he* *takes the students to a movie or athletic event. He gives the girls candy and the boys t-shirts. Church leaders think the discipleship program is a good idea, but no one knows any details about the program. Some of the parents have never met the youth pastor since they do not attend church. Some of the single parents think he is great because he serves as a wonderful role model for their children. He even offers to let them stay all night at his apartment if the single parent has to go out of town.*

Scenario 2: *The meetings occur at the church during regular office hours. Other staff members are present in the building. No meeting is one-on-one. Instead, they occur in the church library with the youth pastor and youth members seated at a table. The library door is open and the church receptionist is directly across the hall. The senior pastor has approved the discipleship effort. The schedule of meetings is made through the church receptionist on a monthly basis, and a copy of the schedule is given to the participants, their parents, and the pastor. The youth pastor was screened before being hired, including a criminal records check. The church has a policy that the youth pastor may not individually socialize with any member of the youth group, invite individuals to his home, or give any individual member a gift without the knowledge of the pastor. All parents are asked to sign a permission form before their child can participate in the discipleship program.*

The programs in Scenarios 1 and 2 could both potentially result in very effective and rewarding discipleship efforts. The difference is that Scenario 1 is a high-risk environment that could just as easily result in child sexual abuse with catastrophic results for the child, the child's family, the youth pastor, the church leadership, and the entire congregation.

Let's look at another example:

Example: *First Church sponsors a scouting program for boys. This* *weekend the boys will be at a wilderness campground using pup tents with two persons to a tent.*

Consider the following two scenarios for this example:

Scenario 1: *The Sunday before the campout, the scoutmaster announces to the congregation that they may have to cancel the trip because they still need two men to serve as supervisors. He asks if anyone is interested in helping, and if so, they should contact him following the service. Randy, a single man who began attending the church several weeks ago, volunteers to help. He's excited about being a part of the program and was an eagle scout himself. The scoutmaster also recruits one of his colleagues from work who enjoys the outdoors and has a son of his own who will go on the trip. It turns out the church has exactly enough tents to accommodate two people per tent. Randy shares a tent with a 13-year-old boy. When they arrive at the camp, the boys are given a few hours to go exploring.*

Scenario 2: *Nine boys and three adult supervisors attend the campout. Each of the supervisors has completed a screening form and has been a member of the church for more than six months. Parents of the boys have all attended an orientation meeting. All the boys, parents, and supervisors are asked to sign an honor code, which explains and stipulates a code of behavior that is to be followed while on the trip. When they arrive at the campground, clear instructions are provided concerning where they can go, and under what circumstances. Each supervisor has clearly defined responsibilities. Two boys of the same approximate age are assigned to each tent. One three-person tent is used to accommodate three boys. The adult supervisors also sleep together in a larger tent. A curfew is in effect once lights are out.*

Based on the three risk factors, we recognize that both scenarios represent a high-risk program, with a dynamic, changing risk environment. Isolation is high; the program occurs overnight; the activities represent higher levels of risk; the potential for secrecy exists; and power differences are present. A need exists to lower isolation, increase accountability, balance power, and maintain specific supervision to observe and control activities.

Nothing in Scenario 1 indicates awareness of the three risk factors. The scoutmaster begins with a high-risk activity and makes it worse through his own actions. Rather than lowering isolation, he increases it as the boys go exploring. Rather than increasing accountability, he decreases it by recruiting supervisors that have not been properly screened. Rather than balancing power, he creates an imbalance by having an adult sleep alone with a child in the same tent. Nothing indicates an understanding of the risk of child sexual abuse, or the steps that can be taken to lower that risk.

Scenario 2 reflects fundamental principles of risk management. Isolation is reduced through the use of boundary conditions, including a curfew. The use of an honor code, an orientation meeting, and screening increases accountability. Sleeping arrangements are planned to maintain a balance of power. Even though these measures have been taken, abuse could still occur. But the church has taken significant steps to reduce that risk. If an allegation of negligent supervision occurred, the church would be able to defend itself using a coherent strategy of care grounded in identifiable principles of risk management.

▶ ***Action Item:*** It is important that all ministry leaders be able to assess levels of risk and understand how to lower risk through adjustments in the nature of the supervision that is provided. To practice this, select one or more of your ministry activities. Assess the risk level using the factors of isolation, accountability, and power. Identify steps that can be taken to lower risk.

Fill in the blanks:

The (<u>two-adult</u>) rule is the first principle of supervision.

Three factors that determine the level of risk are (<u>isolation</u>), (<u>accountability</u>), and (<u>power</u>).

When sitting with toddlers, always avoid placing a child in a way that covers your (private areas).

Disparity in power increases as the gap in (age), (size), and level of authority widens.

Introduce and discuss your church's supervisory policies and guidelines. (Be sure to hand out a copy to each person in the group.)

Although these safeguards are easy to understand in concept, their application might produce conflicts or dilemmas for ministry leaders. Allow time for questions and comments. Encourage class members to share their opinions and concerns with each other. Spend sufficient time to make sure each leader understands these policies and procedures.

The risk factors and principles discussed in this chapter provide a basis for supervising activities involving children in order to reduce the risk of child sexual abuse. Ministries should train both paid and volunteer staff members to understand these principles and to apply them as they plan and supervise activities.

○   ○   ○

Ministry leaders need to know how to report a suspected case of child sexual abuse in the church, and how to respond to any allegation that is brought forth. The next video, **"Responding to an Allegation,"** walks you through the best way to handle these situations.

- **View Video #9: "Responding to an Allegation."**

OPEN FOR DISCUSSION:

- Now that you've seen this DVD segment, how would you respond to an allegation?

- How would you have responded to the parents' first phone call about the youth pastor instant messaging their daughter?

- What steps of responding to an allegation would be the hardest for you to enforce, and why?

Going Deeper ○ ○ ◇ ○ ◇ ○

Handling an Incident

Not only must a ministry do all it can to prevent abuse; it must also be prepared to respond if a reported case of abuse should occur. Every worker should be equipped to know when and how to report any suspicious activities. Here are some guidelines that will be helpful in understanding how to handle an incident of sexual abuse in your ministry.

DISCUSS SUSPICIOUS BEHAVIOR IMMEDIATELY

Any inappropriate conduct or relationships between an adult worker and a member of the youth group or a child should be confronted immediately and investigated. Issue a prompt warning, or if necessary, terminate the adult worker's services immediately if the violation is of sufficient gravity. Ministry staff members should note when a student appears aloof or withdrawn, or exhibits a marked personality change. This may indicate a problem that deserves attention.

Some types of conduct only require an initial comment or warning:

> **Example:** *The church youth group is having a picnic at a local lake. Following a volleyball game, one of the male chaperones begins to massage the shoulders of one of the female youth members. They are seated at a picnic table surrounded by other students. A second adult chaperone discretely pulls the first one aside and comments, "You probably weren't aware, but giving massages falls outside of proper volunteer conduct."*

Other types of conduct require immediate reporting:

> **Example:** *The same facts as the preceding example, but the volunteer worker walks the student to an isolated location and massages her shoulders while laying down on the ground next to her. A second volunteer sees what is happening and immediately reports it to the adult in charge.*

> **Example:** *A male youth volunteer is seen kissing a female member of the youth group. The action is immediately reported to the pastor.*

DISCUSS POTENTIAL CRIMINAL SANCTIONS WITH YOUTH WORKERS

Adults who work with children and adolescent youth should understand that sexual relationships with minors could lead to a felony conviction and imprisonment in a state penitentiary. The law views such misconduct very seriously, as it should. Children's/Youth workers also need to understand that the insurance policy will not provide them with a legal defense in the case of a sexual misconduct charge, or pay any portion of a jury verdict assessed against them on account of such conduct.

MONITOR FACILITIES AND CREATE OPEN ENVIRONMENTS

Appoint a person to monitor the facilities during services and activities. Sunday school superintendents or other ministry leaders also should make random visits to all classrooms and frequently visit or inspect areas of the ministry facility that are isolated. If feasible, consider installing windows on the doors to all classrooms or other areas used by minors. The windows should be made out of shatterproof glass. Alternatively, the doors to such classrooms should be left open during use so that persons passing by can observe what is happening inside. Some ministries also use video systems to monitor facilities.

ESTABLISH SAFEGUARDS FOR ARRIVAL AND DISMISSAL

It's necessary to establish guidelines so that children are not left unsupervised prior to or following ministry activities.

USE A NURSERY IDENTIFICATION PROCEDURE

Procedures should exist for the nursery that clearly identifies the child and the child's parent or guardian. Children should only be released to a properly identified and preauthorized adult.

DISCUSS APPROPRIATE AND INAPPROPRIATE TOUCHING

Touching should always be age-appropriate and based on the need of the child, not the need of the adult. Clearly, touching is an important way of showing comfort and affection to small children. But it should only be done in response to the child's need.

> **Example:** *Sarah, a 2-year old, falls down and scratches her knee and begins to cry. Jean, one of the nursery attendants, places Sarah next to her so they can sit close to each other. This is an example of appropriate touching.*

> **Example:** *Paul, an adult youth supervisor, wraps his arms around the waist of a 14-year-old girl at a church youth activity. This is an example of inappropriate touching.*

○   ○   ○

MUTUAL ACCOUNTABILITY—A MINISTRY OBLIGATION

Questionable or inappropriate behavior often precedes acts of child molestation. Ministry workers should be trained to identify inappropriate behavior with children. They should also be encouraged to warn each other when questionable behavior is displayed, and to report such behavior to the proper individuals. Such a policy, if implemented with care and sensitivity, can help to avoid actual instances of abuse or molestation.

PERSONAL RESPONSIBILITY—A MORAL OBLIGATION

Workers sometimes fail to report a suspected incident of child sexual abuse for a variety of reasons. Some may want to avoid embarrassing situations, or a fear of possible personal and legal recrimination may exist. Nevertheless, discrete and confidential reporting of suspected abuse is critical to abuse prevention. Reporting reflects caring and is not an act of disloyalty.

MINISTRY REPORTING PROCEDURE

Your ministry should develop clear instructions concerning when a report should occur and how it should be made.

Here are some additional factors to consider in deciding whether or not to report a particular incident of suspected abuse to the state:

(1) **Are you a mandatory or permissive reporter under state law?** Mandatory reporters (as defined by state law) face criminal penalties for not reporting. Permissive reporters are permitted to report but they are not legally required to do so. However, it is possible that permissive reporters who do not report reasonable suspicions of abuse will be sued later by victims who allege that their suffering was perpetuated by the failure to report. Therefore, do not automatically dismiss a duty to report on the ground that you are a permissive reporter under state law.

(2) **What is the definition of child abuse in my state?** Some states define abuse very narrowly to include only abuse inflicted by a parent or caretaker.

(3) **Do I have reasonable cause to believe that abuse has occurred?** Remember, most state laws require mandatory reporters to report not only actual abuse, but also reasonable suspicions of abuse. Our recommendation—interpret " reasonable cause" very broadly. Also, note that child abusers, when confronted with their misconduct, often deny it. Any allegation must be treated seriously.

(4) **Be especially aggressive when dealing with pedophilic behavior** (that is, sexual molestation of a pre-adolescent child). Some studies suggest that a pedophile may have hundreds of victims over the course of a lifetime. You have a duty to protect other innocent victims. Resolve doubts in favor of reporting.

(5) **Be especially aggressive when dealing with suspected abuse on the part of a person with a history of previous abusive behavior.** Resolve doubts in favor of reporting.

(6) **Does the clergy-penitent privilege apply?** In a few states, clergy who learn of child abuse during a confidential counseling session are not required to report the information to the state.

(7) **Consider discussing the case anonymously with a representative of the state agency that receives reports of abuse.** These representatives often are more than willing to discuss particular cases

and evaluate whether or not a report should be filed. Of course, if you are advised that a report need not be filed, be sure to obtain the representative's name and make a record of the call.

(8) **Consider filing an anonymous report from the office of some independent third party** (such as a local attorney or the pastor of another church). The other person can later verify that you in fact made the report.

(9) **If you have any doubts concerning your duty to report an particular incident to the state, an attorney should be consulted.** It is also desirable to inform your insurance agent.

WHEN YOUR MINISTRY IS ACCUSED OF ABUSE

Realistically, no practical prevention strategy is 100 percent effective, and an accusation of child sexual abuse may occur in any ministry. Review the **"Allegation Response Checklist"** at the back of the Trainee Workbook. Following this checklist, there is also detailed information on the steps you or your child protection team should take to properly handle an allegation of child sexual abuse.

Fill in the blanks:

Any inappropriate (<u>conduct</u>) or relationships between an adult worker and a member of the youth group or a child should be (<u>confronted</u>) immediately and investigated.

Reporting an incident of inappropriate behavior by another leader toward a child reflects (<u>caring</u>) and is not an act of (<u>disloyalty</u>).

Ministry workers should be aware of (<u>state</u>) laws that govern the reporting of child abuse.

▪ **View Video #10: "Take the Next Steps."**

This training is merely a first step toward raising awareness for the importance of protecting kids from sexual abuse, and for practical ways to implement a child protection program.

OPEN FOR DISCUSSION:

- What key take-away points did you gain from the Training DVD?

- After seeing the entire Training DVD, where do you stand in your commitment to safeguard children in your ministry from becoming victims of sexual abuse?

- What obstacles or concerns do you still have about being able to implement a more consistent, thorough approach to screening and supervising workers?

- What changes will you need to make in order to follow the full screening process—including application, interview, references, background checks, and the *Reducing the Risk* training program?

After you have completed all of the Reducing the Risk ***Training DVD*** *segments and have read the* ***Trainee Workbook*** *that pertains to your ministry role, you are ready to take your Test. Please go to the back of the* ***Trainee Workbook*** *and tear out this test. When you have finished it, turn it in to your supervisor. You may be asked to repeat this training periodically.*

CHAPTER FOUR

Training Children's/ Youth Workers

IMPLEMENTING THE PROGRAM WITH STAFF AND VOLUNTEERS

Keeping kids safe is your first priority.

"See that you do not look down on one of these little ones. For I tell you that these angels in heaven always see the face of my Father in heaven. (Matthew 18:10)

You serve in this ministry because you love kids. Nothing satisfies a committed children's worker more than seeing a child grow in Christ. Real spiritual growth can only take place in a safe environment—a place where kids' questions and their journey to God are honored and protected. This child protection training will teach you about the very real problem of child sexual abuse and its devastating effects in faith communities. Thankfully, there is hope. Because of people like you, children in ministry programs everywhere are better protected. The same love that compelled you to answer the call to serve in this ministry is the love that will inspire you to implement the protection policies you'll learn here.

Training Overview

For Children's/Youth Workers (approximately 2 hours)

WHAT'S THE GOAL OF THIS TRAINING?

- To train children's/youth ministry workers on our child protection policies.
- To inspire ministry workers to keep kids safe.

WHO SHOULD ATTEND?

- All workers of programs geared toward children and youth—whether full-time or occasional—should attend this session.

WHAT RESOURCES FROM MY **REDUCING THE RISK** KIT WILL I NEED?

- *Reducing the Risk* Training DVD
- Copies of Church Policy Statement
- *Reducing the Risk* Trainee Workbook for each participant

WHAT ADDITIONAL SUPPLIES WILL I NEED TO LEAD THE TRAINING?

- DVD player and monitor
- Markerboard or flip chart, markers

HOW OFTEN SHOULD WE DO THIS TRAINING?

Plan to schedule at least two major training sessions per year for new workers and for those who need to renew their training. You may want to repeat child protection training on a periodic basis. As you add new staff and volunteers to your ministry team, provide group training as needed. If you are unable to host a group session for these new workers, we suggest ether giving them the Training DVD to view at home while following along in their Trainee Workbook, or sending them to online training at **ReducingTheRisk.com**. (The online training resource is an additional fee.)

Training Step-By-Step

1. LEADER'S PREP

- Be prepared with copies of your ministry's child protection program.

2. GET STARTED

- Introduce yourself to your group and start your training with a brief devotional to focus your ministry workers' thoughts on the topic of protecting kids.

- Today, you'll learn about the problem of child sexual abuse in faith communities and how to keep kids safe from this tragedy. Keeping kids safe is the first priority of children's ministry. If children aren't safe—whether physically, emotionally, mentally, or spiritually—you can't effectively minister to them.

- **View Video #1: "Child Protection as the Foundation of Your Ministry."**

- **View Video #2: "A Victim's Story."**

OPEN FOR DISCUSSION:

- Why did you choose to serve in children's or youth ministry?

- Based on the first two DVD segments, what initial impressions do you have about our efforts to provide a safe environment for children?

- What should children and their parents reasonably expect from us as ministry workers when they participate in our programs?

- How did the **"Victim's Story"** make you feel? What parts of that video segment especially stood out to you?

Fill in the blanks:

When it comes to (child sexual abuse), many people still don't believe that the (danger) is real.

When a child has a good ministry experience, he's more likely to (grow) in his faith and stay involved with the (church/ministry). When a child is a victim of sexual abuse in the faith community, the (effects) are devastating and last the child's (lifetime).

- Our ministry is committed to being the safest place on Earth for children to grow in their faith. The first way we practice this principle is by following a consistent, thorough screening process. The second step we take toward safeguarding kids is establishing policies for supervision. Our next DVD segment will highlight several common scenarios you're likely to encounter in ministry, and you'll have a chance as a group to brainstorm solutions in between each scene.

- **View Video #8: "Supervising Scenarios: What Would You Do?"**

- **The Toddler Room:** What would you do?

- **Preschoolers:** What would you do?

- **Middle Schoolers:** What would you do?

- **High Schoolers:** What would you do?

- Now that you've considered each of the scenarios in the video, let's look at our ministry's supervision policies and guidelines, and expectations for behavior by leaders.

▶ Tip Although these safeguards are easy to understand in concept, their application might produce conflicts or dilemmas for church workers and volunteers. Allow time for questions and comments. Encourage class members to share their opinions and concerns with each other. Spend sufficient time to make sure each leader understands these policies and procedures.

Fill in the blanks:

Our ministry's supervision policies include:

I am expected to:

The three factors that determine the level of risk include (isolation), (accountability), and (power).

- Let's practice using supervision principles on one more scenario. Analyze each situation using the three risk factors of isolation, accountability, and power.

Example: *You serve as a volunteer worker with the high school ministry. The pastor introduces you to Brett, a son of committed church members, who has come home from college to be a summer ministry intern. Three weeks later, your group has a day-long outing at the lake. Several times you notice that, while Brett plays in the lake with a group of kids, a lot of physical contact with several girls occurs. Later in the day you notice Brett giving a neck massage to a girl during a rest period.*

- Does such behavior warrant any response?
- What should you do after witnessing Brett's behavior?

Going Deeper

Reporting Procedures for Ministry Workers

Child sexual abuse thrives when it goes unnoticed or unreported. Often, an abusive situation continues because of someone's failure to report it. As children's/youth workers you need to know what constitutes an occasion for reporting, the reporting channels they should use, and their obligations to make a report.

Reporting Obligations

An effective reporting procedure enhances the effort to protect children. Ordinarily, child molesters will not remain in a church where workers are trained to identify symptoms of child abuse and are encouraged to report suspicious behavior. Child abusers thrive on secrecy and are more likely to commit criminal acts in organizations where they go unnoticed.

STATE COMPLIANCE — A LEGAL OBLIGATION

Every state has a mandatory reporting law that specifies the following:

- What constitutes child abuse.

- Those persons ("mandatory reporters") who are legally responsible for reporting known and reasonably suspected cases of abuse. Most states require a direct report to a state agency.

- The length of time required to make a report. In most states, those providing professional care or services to children have a 48-hour period to make a report. In some states, an oral report is due within 24 hours.

- The nature and content of the report. Many states permit the reporter to remain anonymous. However, if an individual desires to remain anonymous, the report should be made over the phone in the presence of an attorney or other independent witness who can verify later, if necessary, the identity of the reporter. This may become important if the reporter later is charged with negligence for failing to make a report. If no witnesses to the report exist, and the report is done anonymously, providing a defense becomes problematic.

- The social agencies or department to be contacted. In some states, reports can made to law enforcement officers.

- The criminal penalties for failing to report. Failure to report may be punishable by a fine or jail sentence.

- Protection from legal and civil litigation if the report is made in good faith.

> ▶ **Tip** Be sure to check your state child abuse reporting laws regularly. State legislatures tend to amend these laws often, and children's/youth workers need to be aware of any such changes. Richard Hammar publishes an annual state-by-state listing of child sexual abuse reporting laws. Visit *ReducingTheRisk.com* for more information.

o   o   o

- **View Video #9: "Responding to an Allegation."**

- **View Video #10: "Taking the Next Step."**

- In **"Responding to an Allegation,"** Jasmine recounted the steps she and her church took in order to respond to an allegation of an abuse with a youth worker and a young girl. How would you have responded to these allegations?

- Who would you report an incident to if you suspected a child had been abused by a co-worker in your ministry?

- Review your ministry's procedures for reporting an incident and responding to an allegation.

PERSONAL COMMITMENT

Congratulations! You've just completed one of the most important training opportunities of our ministry. Please take a minute to reflect on your personal commitment to protecting children from being abused in our ministry. The final step in your training is to take the test at the back of this book. Please tear it out and turn in your completed test to your supervisor. You may be asked to repeat child protection training periodically.

A responsive reading, prayer, or some other form of personal devotion can be used to solemnize the commitment to provide a safe place for children.

The training session should end with a time of personal commitment. You can also have each participant sign the written policy statement, which includes the date they participated in your child protection training session. Training participants should be instructed to finish their reading in the Trainee Workbook and turn in their completed test to you. Store their test in their **Screening Forms & Records File for Volunteers**.

CHAPTER FIVE

Training Faith Communities

CASTING VISION TO YOUR CONGREGATION

Educating Everyone for a Safer Environment

Dear children, do not let anyone lead you astray. He who does what is right is righteous, just as he is righteous. (1 John 3:7)

A faith community that understands the concerns and issues inherent in the problem of child sexual abuse will endorse and support efforts to reduce this risk. In addition, an educated community will provide future workers who will already be convinced that the ministry's prevention plan is a necessary and vital safeguard for children.

Your entire faith community needs to understand the nature of this risk and why you have adopted worker screening and other safeguards. This critical information should be communicated in a variety of ways and repeated over time to ensure that as many people as possible grasp the rationale for your prevention efforts.

As a faith community addresses the issue of child sexual abuse, a variety of related issues and concerns may emerge. For example, adult survivors of child sexual abuse often seek support concerning the issues they face and how they can start along the path of healing and recovery. Parents may ask for information regarding how to help their children resist the advances of a molester. Other individuals may request training to help them assist families in their communities that have been victimized in some way by sexual abuse.

There are plenty of opportunities to share pertinent information with the people in your pews and programs. Here are several examples of ways you can help cast the vision for your child protection program:

SPECIAL EMPHASIS DAY

Make child safety a theme for a Sunday. This could be part of a series that focuses on social issues, or it could stand alone as a worship theme. A special speaker, the sermon, bulletin inserts, a joint session of adult Sunday School or religion classes are all ways to instruct the church family. Sections of the *Reducing the Risk* **Training DVD** can be shown as a stimulating way to present information to your faith community during this day.

ADULT EDUCATION CLASSES

Child sexual abuse could be an excellent topic for a special adult Sunday school or education class. The *Reducing the Risk* resources kit could be used with other materials to provide a 4–6 week class for interested adults.

MEMBERSHIP ORIENTATION

If your faith community sponsors a new member's class or a class for visitors, take a few minutes to share about your ministry's efforts to provide a safe place for children. Provide a basic overview of the program. This will likely reap benefits, as parents are looking for churches that take safety seriously. In addition, having an abuse-prevention program will attract new members and provide assurance to those families who are new to the community.

Resources

STATISTICS & QUOTES

This section contains additional illustration material for instructional use.

- The first child sexual abuse lawsuit was filed against a church in 1984. Since then, hundreds of claims have been filed resulting in millions of dollars of expenses.

- "Sexual abuse occurs when dependent, developmentally immature children and adolescents become involved in sexual activity which they do not understand fully and to which they cannot freely give informed consent" (Sean Sammon, *Slayer of the Soul*, p. 6).

- "Child sexual abuse is any sexual act or sexual contact with a child performed by an adult or an older child. It also includes showing an adult's genitalia to a child, showing the child pornographic pictures or videotapes, or using the child as a model for pornographic purposes" (*Protecting Our Children— Sexual Abuse of Children Is Going On, and Too Often Undetected*).

- In 2001, approximately 903,000 children were found to be victims of child maltreatment. Maltreatment categories typically include neglect, medical neglect, physical abuse, sexual abuse, and psychological maltreatment. More than half of child victims (57 percent) suffered neglect; 2 percent suffered medical neglect; 19 percent were physically abused; 10 percent were sexually abused; and 7 percent were psychologically maltreated (National Clearinghouse on Child Abuse and Neglect).

- "Contrary to popular belief, perpetrators of sexual abuse are well known to the child in 85 percent of reported cases. This statistic dispels the myth that only strangers molest children" (Delaplane, D. and Delaplane, A., *Victims of Child Abuse, Domestic Violence, Elder Abuse, Rape, Robbery, Assault, and Violent Death: A Manual for Clergy and Congregations*).

- In one study done in 1989, 453 pedophiles were found to have committed in their lifetimes 106,916 acts of child molestation against 67,112 different victims. That is an average of 236 victims per molester!

- One in three sexual assault victims is under the age of 12. forty three percent of those are six and younger, 34 percent are 7 to 11 (National Center for Victims of Crime).

- A 1996 National Institute of Justice study estimated that each year child sexual abuse in America costs the nation $23 billion. Ninety to ninety-five percent of all sexual abuse cases are never reported to the police.

- "Who are the abusers? Although many parents fear the unknown 'molester,' a child is actually much more likely to be abused by someone he or she knows. An abuser can be anyone caring for a child: a parent or other relative, a baby-sitter, a teacher, a neighbor, or a friend" (American Medical Association, *Child Abuse and Neglect*).

- "A history of childhood sexual abuse leads to a lower health-related quality of life and a greater number of health problems, psychiatric symptoms, and diagnoses. Research shows that survivors of childhood sexual abuse have 'more medical problems, higher medical use, more physical symptoms, lower health status, and more medical procedures'" (American Psychological Association, *Understanding Child Sexual Abuse: Education, Prevention, and Recovery*).

- Children with disabilities are 4 to 10 times more vulnerable to sexual abuse than their non-disabled peers (National Resource Center on Child Sexual Abuse, 1992).

- "As much as 56 percent of reported child molestation cases are committed by adolescents, mostly male" (Roger Katz, "Psychosocial Adjustment in Adolescent Child Molesters" in *Child Abuse and Neglect*, Vol. 14, 1990).

- Between 1986 and 1996, the estimated number of sexually abused children increased 83 Percent (National Center on Child Abuse and Neglect).

- In the December 2, 1998, issue of *The Journal of the American Medical Association*, authors reviewing the literature on child sexual abuse found that sexual victimization of boys and male adolescents is common, but often goes unreported and untreated. Boys at highest risk for abuse are less than 13 years old, non-white, of low socio-economic status, and not living with their fathers. The authors report that the perpetrators tended to be males who were known by, but usually unrelated to, the victims. The abuse typically occurred outside the home and was often repeated.

- "Most sexual offenders are male. One in four offenders is a member of the child's family or a person who has been entrusted with the care of the child. Approximately half are friends of the child or family" (*Child Sexual Abuse: Guidelines for Community Workers*, p.23).

ADDITIONAL RESOURCES

The following resources will be of great value to you and your ministry in its ongoing effort to reduce the risk of child abuse and help your ministry to develop as a learning community in the area of risk management.

The Risk Management Handbook for Churches and Schools

The *Risk Management Handbook* provides vital safety information that touches every aspect of ministry life. The book contains 34 chapters covering nearly 500 pages of material. For more information, visit the online bookstore at **ReducingTheRisk.com** and review the risk management resources.

Inspection Checklists

Inspection and safety checklists are available to assist your church in developing a comprehensive safety program. These checklists complement the *Risk Management Handbook.* For more information, visit the online bookstore at **ReducingTheRisk.com** and review the risk management resources.

Preventing Child Sexual Abuse Test (with Answers):

Please indicate whether the following statements are true or false.

1. Child sexual abuse always involves physical contact with children. **(false)**
2. Most child molesters are male. **(true)**
3. Child molesters are usually strangers to the victim. **(false)**
4. Victims of sexual abuse suffer no long-term effects. **(false)**
5. Most ministries screen workers for potential molesters. **(false)**
6. Ministry leaders cannot be held liable for child sexual abuse. **(false)**
7. A child molester who has experienced a religious conversion no longer presents a threat to children. **(false)**

Choose the correct answers for the following questions.

10. Which of the following are risk factors as they pertain to supervision?

   a) isolation

   b) arrogance

   c) small rooms

   d) accountability

   e) power

   (a, d, e)

11. When a child has been abused, or an accusation has been made, what are the ministry's next steps?

   a) take it seriously

   b) document the allegation

   c) take it to a state agency

   d) provide support for the victim

   e) all of the above

   (e)

12. *(For Ministry Leaders only)* What four steps should every ministry take during the screening process?

    a) personal interview

    b) give a written test

    c) reference checks

    d) written application

    e) observe applicant with children

    f) background check

    (a, c, d, f-optional)

Answer the following questions. (For Ministry Leaders only)

13. What makes a ministry susceptible to sex offenders?

(Churches tend to be child-nurturing environments with few barriers that prevent easy access to children.)

14. Who do sex offenders "groom" as discussed in the Round-Table video segment?

(Predators groom both children and the adult community.)

15. What is one thing you've learned about ministry liability concerning child sexual abuse?

(Correct answers could include: theories of liability—negligent screening, selection, and retention; churches must uphold a reasonable standard of care as established by other youth-serving organizations in the community.)

Appendix 1

SAMPLE FORMS

The following forms contain basic information you may want to use to document ministry policies and procedures for different aspects of your child sexual abuse prevention program. Each form may be used as-is or may be customized to include relevant information for your ministry. Have an attorney review all of your forms and procedures.

Child Protection Plan

What we believe

We believe it is our responsibility to protect the children in our care. Children (and parents) need to know that we have taken every reasonable step to ensure children's safety in our ministry.

We believe it is our responsibility to protect staff and volunteer workers in our ministry from being exposed to false accusations of sexual misconduct. To this end, we have screening and supervision policies in place to protect our ministry workers.

We believe it is our responsibility to protect our ministry. By requiring child protection training, as well as implementing screening and supervision policies, we are modeling good safety procedures to others who look to our ministry as an example of a well-run ministry to children and youth.

What we require

1. **The six-month rule.** The purpose of this rule is to prevent predators from gaining quick access to potential victims. A predator will not want to spend an extended period of time waiting to gain access to children, especially when he can go elsewhere and have almost immediate access. Six months provides a threshold of time for individuals to become better known, and gives an opportunity to evaluate their suitability for volunteer service. In some cases, this length of time is reduced based on a person's ability to provide positive character references from other youth-serving organizations and from our ministry leaders, and a person's prior history working with children in a previous faith community.

2. **A written application.** We require a written Volunteer Service Application before approving individual for service in our children's/ youth ministry. We want to be sure we're selecting the best candidates possible for our ministry programs.

3. **Reference checks.** Once the written application is complete, we conduct reference checks. Applicants should indicate that they have been a member of the church for a minimum length of time, such as six months, and should list two or more prior service references, preferably from a youth organization, plus personal references from two or more church members.

4. **A personal interview.** We use the interview time to explore more fully why a candidate wants to work with children or youth. We also review our ministry's policies and procedures regarding the supervision of children.

5. **Additional background checks.** We conduct a criminal records check for all paid staff and clergy who will have access to children. We may conduct criminal records checks on children's/youth workers who

serve with minors. If you will be driving as part of your ministry service with minors, we will require you to complete a driving information form.

What we expect

- **Training**—We expect all staff and volunteers to successfully complete our Child Sexual Abuse Prevention Training program.

- **Appropriate physical contact**—No one should ever feel uncomfortable in the way they are being touched. Appropriate touching means offering a gentle touch on the shoulders, hands, arms, head, or back.

  Inappropriate touching would include kissing, demanding kissing or hugs, touching of the chest, waist, stomach, bottom, or private areas, or any physical contact that feels uncomfortable or violating. Toddlers and older children should never be allowed to sit in your lap, covering your private area. Instead, have a child sit beside you.

- **Responding to inappropriate or suspicious behavior**—All staff and volunteers should report any inappropriate or suspicious behavior to a ministry staff leader immediately. This includes reporting any suspected abuse being committed by another worker, as well as any child who presents signs of abuse. No one will ever be in trouble for reporting suspected abuse.

- **Follow supervision policies.** Our policies are designed to reduce isolation, increase accountability, and reduce the disparity of power between a worker and a child in our program. We expect all children's/youth workers to follow the supervision policies we have in place to accomplish these goals.

I have read and understand these ministry protection guidelines.

_____   _____

Name   Date

Report of Suspected Incident of Child Abuse

Documentation plays an important role in substantiating a complaint. When a complaint is received, the following information should be collected and confidentially maintained. Collecting this information does not relieve you from your obligation to report an incident to the proper state agency. Along with informing your ministry's leadership about an incident, be sure to consult with an attorney to learn your reporting obligation.

1. Name of worker (paid or volunteer) observing or receiving statement of child abuse:

2. Victim's name: Victim's Age/Date of Birth:

3. Date/location victim first came forward with disclosure:

4. Victim's statement (provide detailed summary):

5. Name of person accused of abuse:

   Relationship of accused to victim (paid staff, volunteer, family member, other):

6. Reported to pastor:

   Date/time: Summary:

7. Call to local children and family service agency:

   Date/time: Contact name:
   Summary:

8. Call to victim's parent/guardian:

Date/time: Contact name:
Summary:

9. Call to ministry attorney:

    Date/time: Contact name:
    Summary:

10. Call to insurance company:

    Date/time: Contact name:
    Summary:

11. Call to denominational leader:

    Name: Date/time:
    Summary:

12. Call to law enforcement agency:

    Name: Date/time:
    Summary:

13. Other evidence that supports the allegation (eyewitnesses, medical exams, confessions, etc.).

Signature of person filing report: _____

Date: _____

Appendix 2

RESPONDING TO AN
ALLEGATION

When Your Ministry Is Accused of Abuse

STEP 1: UNDERSTAND THE PROBLEM

Sexual misconduct within ministries now poses a serious threat to every faith community. Few ministry leaders know how to respond when allegations of sexual misconduct occur. Often, the initial response is disbelief, followed by panic.

A thoughtful and caring response to allegations of sexual misconduct can greatly reduce the trauma, both to the victim and to the ministry. An uninformed response, however, can inflict additional pain and alienation, and sow the seeds for legal action against the ministry. Be aware that not all sexual misconduct involves physical contact or touching. Child sexual abuse, for example, may include the use of pornography or watching sexual activity. Sexual misconduct encompasses a broad range of actions, and they all count as abuse.

ESTABLISH A LINE OF REPORTING

Ministry leaders should institute a line of reporting that must be followed in every case of suspected abuse. Reports of possible child abuse should be quickly communicated to the proper ministry leader and to the required state agency. Such reports reflect a serious obligation at the highest levels of ministry leadership, which means that no report should ever be lost in "middle management." All staff and workers should be informed of their reporting obligation mandated by each state.

STEP 2: PROVIDE A CARING RESPONSE

Ministry leaders can receive allegations of sexual misconduct in many different forms and from a variety of sources. In almost all cases, both the sharing and the receipt of such information is a troubling, difficult experience. Emotions run high, and an untrained leader can take a bad situation and quickly make it worse. On the other hand, a leader prepared to receive such information can provide responses and initiate actions that will be helpful to everyone involved.

The following suggestions can assist in providing a helpful response.

- First, be prepared mentally to receive an allegation. Do not express disbelief or respond in any way that minimizes the complaint or places blame upon the complainant. Table 1 provides examples of appropriate and inappropriate responses.

■ Second, be prepared for intense emotions from the complainant. Probing, but sensitive, questions will be necessary to uncover some details. Don't try to form conclusions concerning the truth of the complaint at this time. Rather, emphasize three simple points: (1) that the complaint is being taken seriously, (2) that procedures exist for such complaints and that they will be followed to ensure proper follow-through, and (3) that the ministry desires to extend care and support in whatever ways possible to the victim and the victim's family.

TABLE 1: RESPONDING TO ALLEGATIONS OF SEXUAL MISCONDUCT		
Focus of Conversation	Appropriate Responses	Inappropriate Responses
The initial sharing of the sexual misconduct	■ Thank you for sharing. ■ I know how hard this must be for you. ■ You've done the right thing in sharing this.	■ I can't believe it. ■ This seems impossible. ■ You're not making this up, are you?
Identification of the alleged perpetrator	■ I want you to know that we take your allegation seriously.	■ Are you sure this isn't a case of mistaken identity? ■ I know him; I can't believe he would do such a thing.
Facts about the misconduct	■ I'm very sorry about what has happened. ■ We want to do everything within our power to help and support you.	■ It doesn't sound like that much happened. ■ Don't you feel like you share some of the blame? ■ Why didn't you tell someone earlier? ■ You should have stopped him.
What next?	■ We have procedures in place to respond to allegations, and we want to make certain that nothing like this ever happens again. ■ You have taken a courageous step today. ■ I know it has been difficult, but you've done the right thing.	■ This is going to ruin our church. ■ Have you thought through the implications of this allegation? ■ You must forgive and forget. ■ You've put me in a difficult spot.

STEP 3: DOCUMENT THE ALLEGATION

Using the Checklist on page 117, be sure you follow your ministry's policies for documenting information at the time the allegation is made.

STEP 4: SEEK PROFESSIONAL ASSISTANCE

Contact your insurance company as soon as an allegation is made. Few ministry leaders have experience in dealing with allegations of sexual misconduct. Once an allegation occurs, you should seek professional assistance.

STEP 5: PROVIDE SUPPORT TO THE VICTIM

It is imperative for ministry leaders to "do the right thing" following an incident of abuse or molestation. Tragically, ministry leaders often respond inappropriately to such incidents, and this not only "re-victimizes the victim," but also dramatically increases the risk of litigation.

Assure the victim that:

- The ministry takes very seriously any allegation of sexual misconduct.

- The ministry does not tolerate incidents of sexual misconduct and considers such incidents to be unscriptural, subjecting the perpetrator to discipline.

- The complaint will be investigated immediately and thoroughly.

- The ministry will not tolerate any retaliation against a victim (or family) for filing a complaint, no matter how it is resolved.

STEP 6: FULFILL STATE REPORTING OBLIGATIONS

If child sexual abuse has occurred, or you expect that it has occurred, a report to the state may be required. By reporting the abuse, you are turning the case over to the civil authorities for their independent investigation. Other steps involved in responding to an allegation include deciding how to deal with the alleged perpetrator, informing the congregation, and responding to the media. These details are following in this appendix.

STEP 7: DECIDE ON OPTIONS REGARDING THE ALLEGED PERPETRATOR

Do not contact the alleged perpetrator until the police or the Department of Social Services investigator gives you permission to do so. Otherwise, the perpetrator may try to influence the testimony of the victim, or even flee.

One of the major decisions that must be made following an initial complaint is what restrictions, if any, should be placed upon the alleged perpetrator of the abuse. While the focus below is on ministry employees, the same principles apply to volunteer workers.

EMPLOYMENT OPTIONS CONCERNING PAID MINISTRY STAFF, INCLUDING CLERGY

Do nothing. The individual continues to function as if no allegation had been made. This represents the greatest legal risk to the faith community if the allegation is determined to be true, and the individual continues to engage in sexual misconduct. Punitive damages could potentially be assessed against both the ministry and its leaders.

Restrict the individual's activities. While the complaint is being investigated, the ministry may limit the individual to low-risk activities that pose little threat of sexual misconduct. While this does not eliminate all risk, it does reduce it.

Place the individual on a paid or unpaid leave of absence. In this case, if the allegations are substantiated, dismissal will normally occur. If the allegations are found to be false, the individual should be reinstated. If the findings are inconclusive, the individual may or may not be reinstated, based upon the totality of the evidence. If reinstatement does occur, additional restrictions should be considered concerning contact with minors. A number of scenarios are presented in the following section.

FACTORS TO CONSIDER REGARDING EMPLOYMENT OPTIONS

If the alleged perpetrator is a paid staff member of the ministry, then leaders face the question of whether or not to terminate the employee.

The following factors should be taken into account in making that decision.

- If the abuse is reported to civil authorities, the alleged offender should he removed from any position involving contact with minors, pending the investigation by civil authorities. The safety and welfare of all involved should be carefully maintained.

- If the accused confesses to an incident of sexual molestation or sexual seduction, then termination of employment is in order. Remember, retaining such a person (giving him or her a "second chance") imposes extraordinary legal risk upon the ministry, for it will make the ministry vulnerable to a charge of "negligent retention" in the event the perpetrator repeats the sexual misconduct. Such an employee should not be retained without the express advice of competent legal counsel.

- If the accused does not confess, then the ministry needs to proceed carefully, since it can be sued for "wrongful termination" if it dismisses the accused on the basis of insufficient evidence. If there is clear and convincing evidence of guilt, then the ministry is free to dismiss the employee with little fear of legal retaliation. The dismissed employee may sue the ministry, but such a case would be very unlikely to succeed if the ministry in fact has clear and convincing evidence of guilt. Further, note that juries will view the faith community sympathetically in such a case. After all, it was acting to protect children or its members, and any doubt concerning the propriety of its conduct ordinarily will be decided in favor of the faith community rather than the alleged perpetrator.

- If the accused is prosecuted, found guilty, and incarcerated, the ministry under no circumstances should allow that person to resume any position involving contact with minors following his or her release from prison.

- If the accused is prosecuted, found guilty, but not incarcerated— or pleads guilty to a lesser offense—he or she should not be allowed to resume any position involving contact with minors.

- If the accused is prosecuted and found innocent, the ministry may or may not retain the employee. For example, a person may be found not guilty based on criminal standards of evidence (guilt beyond a reasonable doubt), but later found at fault in a civil trial with a different standard of evidence (preponderance of the evidence). Ministry leaders must carefully weigh all the evidence and make a decision concerning the accused worker's future position with the ministry that reflects the evidence and the best interests of the ministry and its members. Three basic options exist: (1) the individual resumes duties exactly as before; (2) the individual resumes duties with new restrictions and boundaries; or (3) the individual resigns or is terminated. The option selected will vary from one situation to another based upon the individual circumstances in each case.

- If the charges are dropped, ministry representatives should frankly discuss the case with the investigating detective in order to determine whether or not the final disposition of the case was based on inconclusive evidence. There are many other reasons— some having nothing to do with the guilt or innocence of the accused—that can lead to a decision not to prosecute, a plea bargain, or an acquittal. Also, a civil case could still occur.

In some cases, the accused denies any wrongdoing and any evidence regarding his or her guilt is inconclusive. In such a case, the ministry has a number of options, including the following:

- Do not dismiss the employee or take any additional actions. This response is appropriate if the accusation is obviously frivolous.

- Do not dismiss the employee, but issue a warning that he or she will be monitored, and that if any additional evidence of impropriety is received by the ministry, the employee will be subject to discipline (which may include dismissal). If a decision is made not to dismiss the employee, then the ministry should advise the alleged victim and the victim's family that: (1) it has investigated the charge thoroughly; (2) the allegation was not established by the evidence; (3) charges of sexual misconduct are very serious, and the ministry cannot find an accused person guilty without clear evidence; (4) there will be no adverse consequences to the alleged victim for filing the complaint; (5) the alleged victim should be encouraged to report immediately any additional evidence, or any further incidents of misconduct; and (6) it is the policy of the ministry, based on its understanding of Scripture, to eliminate sexual misconduct from all of its programs and activities.

- Suspend the employee (with or without pay), pending the outcome of any ongoing investigation. This assumes that the alleged molestation or seduction was reported to the state or a ministry judicatory agency, which in turn initiated an investigation. If the employee is prosecuted and found guilty, then the ministry ordinarily should dismiss him or her. If the employee is acquitted, then ministry leaders should consult with the prosecuting attorney or investigating detective to determine the sufficiency of the evidence. Of course, a ministry should allow the accused employee to confront any witness the ministry uses to support a finding of guilt. In other words, if the ministry asks the prosecuting attorney or investigating detective to appear before the ministry board, the employee also should be present (or invited to attend).

All allegations of sexual misconduct should be treated similarly. Sometimes, ministries treat female employees differently than male employees. Failure to treat similar cases similarly can result in a civil lawsuit against the ministry based on charges of discrimination.

STEP 8: RESPOND TO FAITH COMMUNITY CONCERNS

How and when information is shared with the faith community depends on the unique circumstances of each case. Often the decision is tied to if and when restrictions are placed upon a ministry worker, or if the allegation has become public knowledge. A response may be required following the initial complaint, or it may not occur until after the investigation and a finding has been made. In communicating sensitive information, leaders must be concerned not to engage in the invasion of privacy or defamation. Also, every ministry leader should be familiar with the concept of "qualified privilege." When sensitive information needs to he shared, it should be done in a proper setting that only includes church members.

Cases involving sexual misconduct involve very personal and sensitive information. Maintaining confidentiality ranks as a high priority for all leaders involved. Often, however, allegations of sexual misconduct require that a staff member take a leave of absence during the investigation. That may be for a few days or a few months. Or, if a staff member must be terminated, faith community members may be misinformed or have no idea of why the dismissal occurred. People might view leaders as acting indiscriminately and believe their actions reflect poor judgment, or worse. In these situations, supporters and friends of the dismissed staff member can be ruthless in their attacks upon ministry leaders. Ministry leaders want to clarify their actions to the faith community, but are afraid that if they do so, they may be sued for defamation or invasion of privacy. Some ministry leaders throw caution to the wind and defend themselves and their actions as they describe the sordid details of the misconduct during public services.

Both extremes—to say nothing or to announce everything to everybody—miss the mark and make the situation worse. To say nothing creates suspicion and a backlash that jeopardize the ministry. To say everything can put the ministry and its leaders at legal risk. Fortunately, the courts have addressed this issue and a third, more desirable alternative exists.

The qualified privilege
In some cases, it is advisable for the ministry board to inform the members of incidents of sexual misconduct occurring on ministry property or in the course of ministry activities. Communication like this should be done in such a way that it is protected by a "qualified privilege." This means that the information shared cannot be considered defamatory unless it is made with legal malice, meaning that the persons who communicated the information either knew that it was false, or shared the information with a reckless indifference as to its truth or falsity. Ministry leaders must be careful, though, concerning

how the information considered a "qualified privilege" is communicated. *NOTE: It's best to consult with an attorney before you proceed with this option.*

In some cases, it is helpful to obtain a signed confession from an accused person who has been found guilty or who has confessed. If the accused consents to the communication of the confession to members of the faith community, then you can quote from the confession in a letter that is sent to members of the congregation, or in a membership meeting. Be sure that this consent is in writing.

Often, congregational members will desire more information. The board should designate one person to handle questions, and that person should fully understand the concept of qualified privilege and only disclose information when a common interest has been fully established. Any disclosure should be strictly confidential and on a need-to-know basis.

STEP 9: RESPOND TO THE MEDIA

A case of child sexual abuse in a ministry often results in extensive media coverage. Designate a spokesperson for your faith community, and refer all requests for information to that individual. Your spokesperson should be able to communicate the ministry's concern for all victims of child sexual abuse, and that the ministry takes all allegations seriously. The spokesperson should also understand the legal concerns associated with making public comments and be briefed by the ministry's attorney before meeting with the media.

Also, develop a clear position statement for your ministry regarding child sexual abuse. This statement can be released if an allegation of abuse occurs. Having a carefully prepared statement is far superior to making no comment. This is your opportunity to influence public opinion positively by emphasizing your awareness of the problem of child abuse, your concern for victims, and the extensive steps your ministry has taken to reduce the risk and provide a safe environment for children. This is no time for silence or "no comment." Take the initiative in maintaining a positive public image for your ministry.

Appendix 3

ALLEGATION
RESPONSE CHECKLIST

Allegation Response Checklist

If your ministry is accused of child sexual abuse, use the following checklist to ensure that your response is appropriate and legal.

☐ We have prepared in advance for an allegation of sexual misconduct should one ever occur.

☐ We have taken all allegations seriously, and have not engaged in denial, minimization, or blame. We have followed up on all allegations.

☐ We collected in writing all relevant information concerning the allegation.

☐ We promptly fulfilled any state reporting obligation concerning the alleged child abuse.

☐ We notified our insurance agent, appropriate judicatory leaders, and our attorney concerning the allegation.

☐ We have placed appropriate restrictions on alleged perpetrators of misconduct until the case is resolved.

☐ We have maintained strict confidentiality concerning all information, and will communicate with congregational members on the basis of their need to know under the restrictions of a qualified privilege.

☐ We are providing support to the victim and the victim's family.

References

■ *Breach of Trust Breach of Faith:* Child Sexual Abuse in the Church and Society. Publication services of the Canadian Conference of Catholic Bishops, 90 Parent Avenue, Ottawa, Ontario KIN 7B 1.

■ Conte, John R. *A Look at Child Sexual Abuse.* National Committee for Prevention of Child Abuse Chicago, 1986.

■ *Decree On Child Abuse: Policies, Procedures, and Recommendations.* The Archdiocese of Cincinnati, 100 East Eight Street, Cincinnati, OH 45202, (513) 421-3131.

■ Finkelhor, D., Hotaling, U., Lewis, I., and Smith., C. "Sexual Abuse in a National Survey," *Child Abuse and Neglect* (14:19-28), 1990.

■ Fortune, M. Marie. "A Millstone Round the Neck," *Round Table* (Spring) 1990.

■ *Sexual Violence: The Unmentionable Sin.* New York: Pilgrim Press, 1983.

■ Geffner, R. "Current Issues and Future Directions in Child Sexual Abuse," *Journal of Child Sexual Abuse, Vol. 1* (1992).

■ Kendall-Tackett, K., Williams, L. and Finkelhor, D. Paper presented at the American Professional Society on the Abuse of Children, January 1991, San Diego, California 1991.

■ *The Incidence and Prevalence of Child Sexual Abuse: No Easy Answer.* National Resource Center on Child Sexual Abuse. Huntsville, AL, 1992.

■ *Understanding Child Sexual Abuse,* The Office of Public Communications, The American Psychological Association, 750 First Street, NE, Washington DC 20002-4242: [www.apa.org/releases/sexabuse/]

■ van Dam, Carla. *Identifying Child Molesters: Preventing Child Sexual Abuse by Recognizing the Patters of the Offenders.* Binghamton, NY. Haworth Pr Inc, 2001.

■ Wurtele, S., Kvaternick, M. and Franklin, C. "Sexual Abuse Prevention for Preschoolers: A Survey of Parent's Behaviors, Attitudes, and Beliefs." *Journal of Child Sexual Abuse, Vol. 1* (2: 113-127), 1992.

For additional information regarding the issue of child sexual abuse, visit: **ReducingTheRisk.com**

About the Authors

Richard R. Hammar is an attorney and CPA, specializing in legal and tax issues affecting churches and clergy. He is a graduate of the Harvard Law School, and attended Harvard Divinity School. He is the author of *Pastor, Church & Law*, the annually updated *Church and Clergy Tax Guide*, and *The Church Guide to Copyright Law*. He also serves as editor of CHURCH LAW & TAX REPORT and CHURCH FINANCE TODAY. In 1990, he was inducted into the National Association of Church Business Administration Hall of Fame.

Marian V. Liautaud serves as editor for the Your Church Media Group at Christianity Today International. Along with developing and editing all of the resources included in *Reducing the Risk* 3rd edition, she also is an editor for YOUR CHURCH magazine, CHURCH LAW & TAX REPORT, and CHURCH FINANCE TODAY, plus numerous books, websites and newsletters published through the Your Church Media Group.

MAKE THE BEST USE OF THIS RESOURCE

BY USING IT WITH ALL MATERIALS FROM THE FULL KIT

KEEPING YOUR MINISTRY SAFE FROM CHILD SEXUAL ABUSE

KEEPING YOUR MINISTRY SAFE FROM CHILD SEXUAL ABUSE

Reducing the Risk
3rd Edition

PRICING INFORMATION:

ITEM #L324: **Reducing the Risk** *Training DVD* $**69.95**

ITEM #L323: **Reducing the Risk** *Leader's Guide* $**29.95**

ITEM #L322*: **Reducing the Risk** *Trainee Workbook* $**6.50**

ITEM #L321*: **Reducing the Risk** *Screening Forms & Records File for Volunteers* $**4.50**

SPECIAL COMBO OFFERS:

ITEM #L320S: **Reducing the Risk** *Kit* (includes 1 Training DVD, 1 Leader's Guide, 10 Trainee Workbooks, and 10 Screening Forms & Records Files for Volunteers) *SPECIAL OFFER* $**149.95** *(more than a 25% savings)*

ITEM #L322S: **Reducing the Risk** *Trainee Refill* (includes 10 Trainee Workbooks and 10 Screening Forms & Records Files for Volunteers) $**79.95** *(more than a 25% savings)*

ITEM #L323S: **Reducing the Risk** *Leader's Starter Kit* (includes 1 Training DVD, 1 Leader's Guide, 1 Trainee Workbook, and 1 Screening Forms & Records File for Volunteers) $**89.95** *(more than a 15% savings)*

*For discounted packs of 10 visit YourChurchCatalog.com

RICHARD HAMMAR,
J. D., LL.M., CPA

Sourcecode: S8CTBØ1

Order online **YourChurchCatalog.com**   Order by phone **1-800-222-1840**

Train Your Board Members on Legal Issues—In Just 4 Hours!

Most church board members have had little or no training on the vital legal issues your church could face during their term. Since the board is responsible for performing the critical tasks that could prevent your church from being exposed to legal liability, it is crucial that they understand the key legal concepts necessary to best protect your church, and themselves, from harm.

The 4 Hour Legal Training Program is designed to train board members on legal issues in eight convenient 30-minute audio sessions. Richard R. Hammar, J.D., LL.M., CPA and James F. Cobble Jr., Ed. D. present your board with the legal background and understanding of these essential issues:

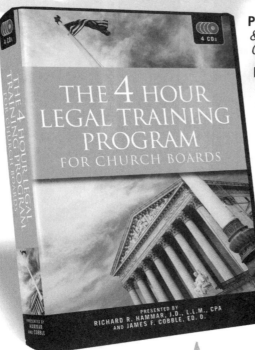

Presentation 1: *Legal Liability & Risk Management for Churches: An Introduction*

Presentation 2: *Legal Liability and Fiduciary Duties*

Presentation 3: *Church Documents and Records*

Presentation 4: *Congregational Issues*

Presentation 5: *Church Financial Issues, Part 1*

Presentation 6: *Church Financial Issues, Part 2*

Presentation 7: *Personnel Issues*

Presentation 8: *Reducing Legal Risk: A Proactive Strategy*

YOUR CHURCH RESOURCES